Denize McIntyre explores a century of education from The School of Mines founded in 1913, to the Polytechnic of Wales, University of Glamorgan and the University of South Wales

ON EQUAL TERMS

University of South Wales
Prifysgol
De Cymru

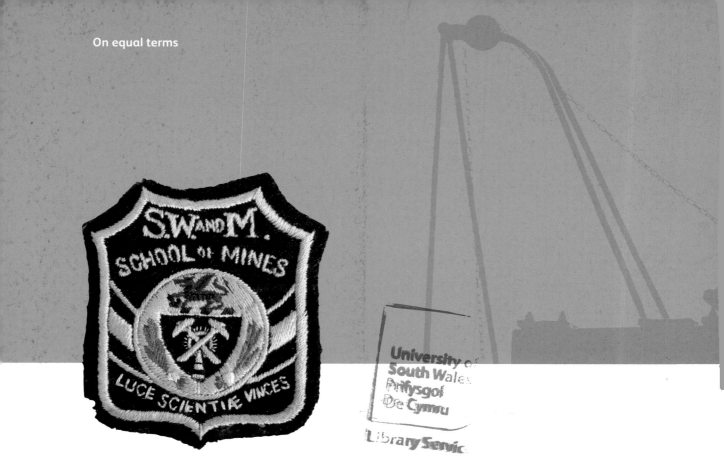

Published by University of South Wales
Autumn 2013. Copyright © University of
South Wales, 2013.
ISBN 978-1-909838-02-4

University of South Wales, Pontypridd,
Wales, United Kingdom CF37 1DL
Tel: 08455 76 01 01
www.southwales.ac.uk

Designed and produced by Graffeg
www.graffeg.com

All photographs and images unless otherwise
stated are © University of South Wales.

Alan Holloway and Rosemary Bailey 108-113;
© Amgueddfa Cenedlaethol Cyrmru/National
Museum of Wales 8, 10, 21, 23, 28, 56, 58, 61,
201; Dr Ceri Thomas 114; East Ayrshire Council
77; Glamorgan Records Office 26, 44, 54, 62;
Graham Pitcher 142; H.J Whitlock and Sons
ltd, © National Portrait Gallery and Llyfrgell
Genedlaethol Cyrmru/National Library Wales &
Alfred Freke (Cardiff), © Llyfrgell Genedlaethol
Cyrmru/National Museum Wales 28, 29, back
cover; Kiran Ridley Photography, cover, title, 7,
14, 17, 37, 52, 78, 81, 83, 86, 87, 92, 105, 115,
116, 118, 132, 139, 145, 148, 162, 172, 174, 182,
183-184, 198-199, 200, 201, 204; Media Wales
Ltd 156; Norman Morris 169-171; Rhondda
Cynon Taf Libraries and Archive Services, cover,
title, 8, 10, 30, 32-33, 35, 40, 46; © South Wales
Evening Post, reproduced by West Glamorgan
Archives Service 88, 106, 122, 123, 124; ©
Victoria and Albert Museum, London 39; Troggs
official website www.my-generation.org.uk 145.

CONTENTS

CHAPTER 1

All students on equal terms

CONTENTS

CHAPTER 4

CHAPTER 5

FOREWORD

Vice Chancellor

Welcome to our celebration of 100 years of education at the University of Glamorgan. This birthday comes at a singularly important time in our history. As I write, we have already become the University of South Wales and our community is happily looking forward to the future. However, such a birthday is a time for reflection and a chance to take pleasure in achievements. Each member of this community, past and present, has their own feelings about the place and some of these views are beautifully expressed in this book and I would like to tell you what it means to me.

Professor Julie Lydon

I feel an immense pride in my University: it has achieved so much but retained all of its original philosophy and aims. I love the sense of energy and purpose; the deep feeling of a community 'belonging'. I've wondered where this came from and concluded that it's from the people – staff and students - as they clearly have self-confidence about what they do, with little time for any with pretentions. My sense is that as the institution had nothing handed to it, everything was hard-earned; this has engendered a sense of 'right' and conviction. The stunning physical environment of the University certainly helps, too. Putting it simply, the place makes my heart swell.

Denize asked me whether all eight Principals, or Heads, have anything in common. Of course we do: it's that we are all guardians of this great place and we work to ensure it has a future. We hand it on, and each of us in our own time operates in a business-like way. I've been really fortunate: I haven't had to manage through world wars or crises of that scale, but the economic downturn of recent years presents challenges for us and our communities. Looking ahead, as we do on birthdays, I believe we'll see changes to the economy and a fundamental change in how higher education is funded; we may even see a new kind of binary divide emerge in which some universities specialise in three-year traditional degrees, whilst others develop a new inter-leaving of work and study for the purposes of affordability and employability. I was also asked how a historian writing the next volume might evaluate me, as Head. That's a difficult thing to answer – but I truly hope I'm remembered for caring about people: students, staff and the communities in which we stand. I'd also like to be thought of as continuing the best traditions whilst planning effectively for the future.

Making predictions is tricky and probably best avoided, but one thing I'm sure of is that the University of South Wales will meet any challenge. It's what we do.

Julie Lydon

> **4 November 1912**

11 Coal Companies indicated their agreement to funding the School of Mines.

17 January 1913

Professor George Knox appointed Principal of the new School of Mines.

8 October 1913

The first cohort of students was enrolled and the first academic year commenced. 29 Full-time and 110 part-time students.

5 October 1914

Second campus of the School of Mines opened at Crumlin, Monmouthshire, under Professor Knox's leadership. 40 part-time students enrolled.

1915

First official inspection of the School of Mines at Treforest took place.

21 August 1915

Ernest Alfred Morgan, aged 24, became the School of Mines' first casualty in World War I (Gallipoli). He was studying Mine Surveying as a part-time day student.

Timeline

24 January 1914

Sir W T Lewis, Baron Merthyr of Senghenydd performed the official opening ceremony.

24 July 1914

South Wales Mining Students Tour returned to Wales from Germany – just 11 days before the declaration of war.

4 August 1914

War declared – significant disruption to the School of Mines.

22 August 1915

David Evans, aged 24, became the School of Mines' second casualty in World War I (Gallipoli). He was studying Mining as a part-time day student.

1916

First official inspection of the School of Mines at Crumlin took place.

1920

The famous beam engine arrived on campus from its location at a closed colliery in Graig, Pontypridd. It almost certainly arrived in train trucks through the tunnel, now part of the campus.

>

1912-1920

On equal terms

> ## 1921

A major period of industrial disputes in South Wales coalfield caused major loss of income to the School of Mines.

1926

The General Strike meant a major loss of income to the School of Mines' funding coal companies.

A joint inspection of the School of Mines at Treforest and Crumlin was held during the General Strike.

1931

Professor George Knox retired after 18 years as Principal. Mr Bobby James took over as Principal.

1932

The School of Mines awarded its first HNDs. The School of Mines was only the third college in the UK to offer sandwich awards with a work-based placement.

1934

Recognised by the University of London for BSc (External) in Mining and Mechanical Engineering and for Higher Degrees by research.

Timeline

INDIAN SCHOOL OF MINES
उत्तिष्ठत जाग्रत प्राप्य वरान्निबोधत

The School was used as a model for the establishment of the Indian School of Mines at Dhanbad, the "coal capital of India".

1927

HM Inspectors commended the work of the School and noted that research of national importance was being undertaken, particularly into mine safety.

13 August 1928

The School of Mines at Treforest passed into the control of Glamorganshire County Council. The Crumlin School passed into the control of Monmouthshire County Council.

1939

Outbreak of Second World War: many students leave to take up military service.

1940

The South Wales and Monmouthshire School of Mines changed its name to The School of Mines & Technology.

April 1941

William Ivor Wright was killed in enemy action whilst serving in the Home Guard. He was a part-time surveying student, aged 19.

>

1921-1941

1943

Additional buildings in Rhydyfelin were constructed to take the School of Mines Junior technical courses. These buildings later became Pontypridd College (now Coleg Morgannwg).

15 December 1943

David Allen Evans was killed in action as a Leading Aircraftman in the RAF Volunteer Reserves. He was a full-time Chemical Engineering student, 21.

1944

A former railway line (now a campus car park) was used to store American military vehicles and equipment in preparation for D Day.

A new Mining Education Centre, under the control of the College, opens in Aberaman, Aberdare. This Centre later goes on to become Aberdare Further Education College.

1950

A shortage of teaching space necessitated turning the caretaker's cottage into a chemical engineering laboratory.

1951

New Department of Commerce and Administration opened in a temporary building at Rhydyfelin. Courses included a two-year full-time course in secretarial work.

Timeline

1946

The new academic year saw a 105% increase in full-time students: servicemen returning from World War 2 and enrolling onto specially designed intensive courses.

1948

From October 1948 to 1950, in order to accommodate the enormous increase in student numbers, the Treforest Boys club on Queen Street was used for lectures and as a drawing office.

1949

Diversification of industries required the introduction of a wider range of courses. Reflecting the new portfolio, the School was renamed the Glamorgan Technical College.

1952

Glamorgan Technical College introduced a new HNC in Electrical Engineering joint with Bridgend Technical College.

1954

Building commenced on the first stage of B Block (Brecon) – including new laboratories, students' common room, and more.

1955

The UK's Minister for Education approved plans for Higher Technological Awards – the first degree equivalent awards outside traditional universities.

>

1943-1955

1956

The second stage of Brecon Building (B Block) was completed in April, providing a library, assembly hall and the first refectory.

1958

Regional status of the college was recognized by the Ministry of Education with a new title, 'The Glamorgan College of Technology'.

1960

Transfer of non-advanced vocational courses to the Pontypridd College in Rhydyfelin (Coleg Morgannwg).

1972 and 1973

New buildings opened: Glynneath (G Block), Students Union, Hirwaun (H Block), Library, and upper Refectory (Stilts).

1975

The Polytechnic merged with Glamorgan College of Education (Barry Teacher Training College).

The name was changed to The Polytechnic of Wales.

THE POLYTECHNIC OF WALES
POLITECHNIG CYMRU

Timeline

14

Glamorgan Polytechnic
Politechnig Morgannwg

1964

Council for National Academic Awards was created by Royal Charter – a number of the College's Diploma courses were automatically converted to degree courses.

1967

The first hall of residence was opened to house 100 students on the college campus. Forest Hall.

1970

The College became Glamorgan Polytechnic.

1976

The 30 acre Tyn-y-Wern outdoor sports facility opened.

1977

The County Council decided that Teacher Training would end on the Barry campus; the final intake of students was in October 1978.

August 1981

The Barry campus closed.

>

1956-1981

On equal terms

> **November 1986**

Building began on Phase 2 of the Learning Resource Centre (LRC).

January 1987

Building began on the Recreation (Sports) Centre.

March 1987

A student initiative was launched to raise funds for scholarships for black South African students.

1989

The Recreation Centre completed and opened.

1 September 1990

The Poly became smoke free- with smoking in buildings banned.

13 June 1991

Diana, Princess of Wales, visited the Poly.

Timeline

30 September 1987

First Honorary Degree (Honorary D.Litt.) awarded to Prof John Meurig Thomas, FRS.

October 1987

First MSc Computer Science completions.

The newly extended LRC opened.

September 1992

The Polytechnic is designated as The University of Glamorgan.

1994

The first Chancellor of the University was installed: the Rt Hon Lord Merlyn Rees of Cilfynydd (former Secretary of State for Northern Ireland and Home Secretary).

The Glyntaff campus was established for the Law School and, thereafter, the School of Care Sciences.

1986-1994

On equal terms

2002

The University celebrated its 10th Anniversary and the Rt Hon Lord Morris of Aberavon KG QC was installed as the second Chancellor of the University.

2006

Merthyr Tydfil College joined the University to become the Faculty of Further Education.

2007

The Cardiff (Atrium) campus opened to house the Creative & Cultural Industries faculty.

The Jetstream 31 aircraft arrived at the new Aircraft Maintenance Centre- the first facility of its kind in Wales.

Spring 2010

Julie Lydon was appointed Vice Chancellor: the first woman in such a role in Wales.

11th April 2013

The University of Glamorgan merged with The University of Wales, Newport to form The University of South Wales.

University of South Wales
Prifysgol De Cymru

Timeline

2008

2009

The University was joined by the Royal Welsh College of Music and Drama.

The University opened the UK's first Hydrogen Research and Demonstration Centre at Baglan Energy Park, near Swansea.

The Universities Heads of the Valleys Institute (UHOVI) was established in collaboration with University of Wales, Newport, to offer new learning opportunities to communities in the area.

Treforest Campus

2002-2013

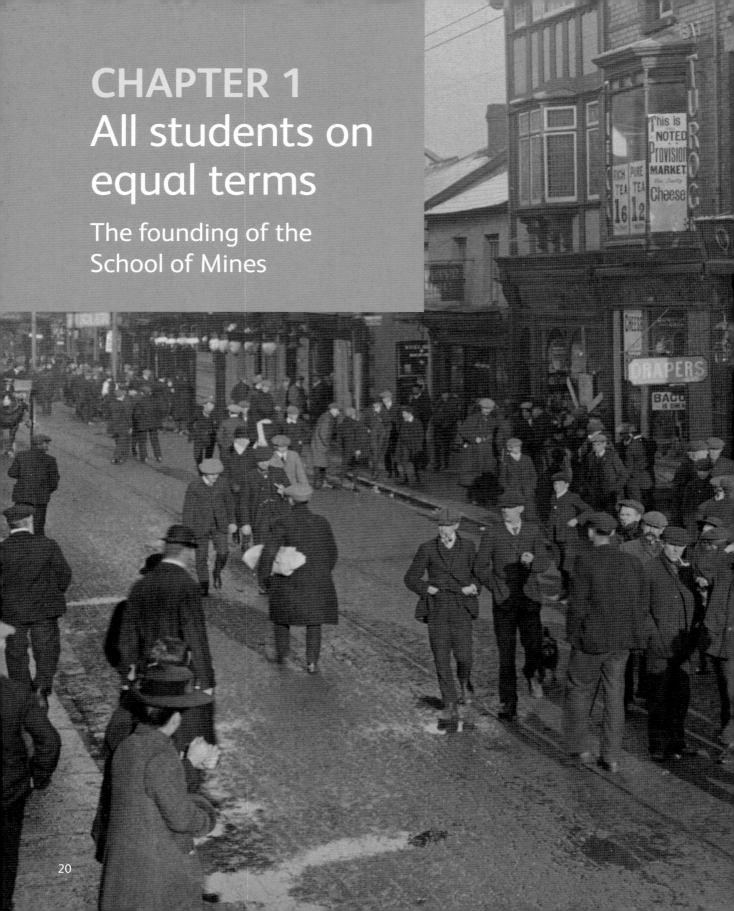

CHAPTER 1
All students on equal terms

The founding of the
School of Mines

Tonypandy 1910-1911

1912

in perspective

The author L.P.Hartley begins his novel *The Go Between* with a line which has become almost a proverb. He writes that 'the past is a foreign country: they do things differently there.'[1] It's an observation full of insight and it couldn't be more relevant to a comparison between the 100 year old University of Glamorgan in 2013 and the brand new South Wales and Monmouthshire School of Mines of 1913. In order to understand this particular foreign country it is important to appreciate as fully as possible the context of the area and the community in which the School was established. This will offer an insight into the 'why' and the 'when' of the origins of the University.

History is littered with eccentrics and radical thinkers; people who are so far in front of the perceived wisdom of their time that they probably appeared bonkers to their contemporaries. There is one such figure in the history of miners' education in South Wales. One of the earliest proposals for establishing a school for the technical education of miners originated with a pioneer called Samuel Baldwin Rogers. Rogers was a founder member of the prestigious South Wales Institute of Engineers and he had some extremely innovative, almost revolutionary ideas for his day. For example, around 1845 he published a pamphlet calling for a toll-free bridge to span the River Severn. Another of his ideas was to lobby for post mortems to be carried out on men who died in mine explosions so the industry might learn precisely what had caused those deaths and how they might better be prevented. In the context of technical education for miners, in 1842 Rogers proposed that a School of Mines be established and that it be funded through a profit-sharing scheme. Even though this radical idea came to fruition somewhat quicker than the Severn Bridge, it was to be a further 71 years before his idea took on a physical shape and the South Wales and Monmouthshire School of Mines opened its doors to students. When it finally did it used a funding model which Rogers would have recognised immediately.

In spite of the forward looking ideas of singular men such as Rogers, South Wales mining communities in the early twentieth century were tough places to live and learn. With small exceptions it was a difficult, depressing and troubled area; there had been some years of significant industrial unrest. Strikes and violent confrontations between coal miners and the police had been

[1] Hartley, L.P. The Go-between Ed. Douglas Brooks-Davies (London: Penguin Modern Classics, 1997), p.5

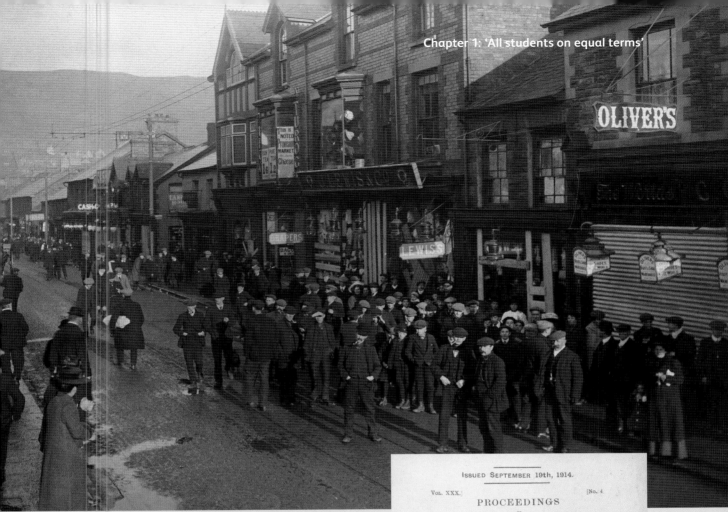

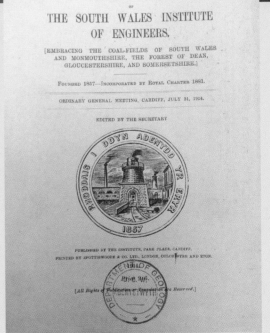

Above: Tonypandy 1910-1911
Right: South Wales Institute of Engineers
proceedings

frequent. The South Wales Federation of Miners (the 'Fed') had a quarter of a million members by 1912 and the coal owners' apparent disregard for the welfare of the men served to increase agitation, resulting in, for example, the Tonypandy miners being joined in their actions by strikers from Cynon Valley collieries, dock-workers at Cardiff and railwaymen at Llanelli. All were resisted by the authorities and many resulted in riots, property damage and even loss of life.

THE OCEAN GRAVE OF THE TITANIC.

LOST LINER'S TRAGEDY.

THE SAILING AND— THE END.

ICE, THE FOE.

SHOCK THAT RENT THE SHIP.

THE BRAVE DEAD.

WOMEN SAVED BY MEN'S SACRIFICE.

THE NOBLE ELEMENT IN THE OCEAN TRAGEDY.

No element of tragedy seems to have failed to contribute its share to the overwhelming catastrophe of the Titanic. The forces of nature shook themselves free from the chains with which Man would bind them, burst in all their power from the limits in which he has sought to confine them, and dealt him a blow that has sent mourning through two nations. His last word in ship construction, equipped with every last device making for safety, or for aid in case of need, met at her maiden issue with the sea a challenge that broke her utterly and took her in toll with over twelve hundred of the lives she carried.

The magnitude of such a disaster leaves the mind as incapable of expressing the emotions aroused in it as its agencies were powerless to avert the catastrophe. For years we take our eager, heedless way, demanding more and more of life, increasingly impatient of its hindrances to our pleasure and our business, increasingly bold and cunning in overcoming them, and never pausing but to congratulate ourselves upon our triumphs. Every now and then comes some cataclysmic reminder that, if it is not possible to go too far and too fast, it is very possible to congratulate ourselves too well. For a brief moment we are brought to a full stop.

We trust the relatives of those who have perished may find some solace in the thought that though they have been called upon to suffer a grief almost unendurable to bear, they suffer it amidst that deepest sympathy which only when we are brought to face the realities of life can be aroused. For us, as for them, moreover, there is heartening thought in one thing that can be read into the disaster from the facts that have come to light. It is terribly clear that scenes of most dreadful horror must have taken place in the few hours between the Titanic's striking and her disappearance. And it is clear, from the fact that women and children form by far the greater majority of the saved, that in this dire emergency the imperilled rose to supreme heights of courage and devotion. Millionaire and steerage emigrant alike were called upon: alike they have presented us with that most inspiring of all spectacles—the inherent nobility of mankind.

The largest ship in the world went to sea from Southampton harbour on the tenth of April, 1912.

People spoke of the tenth of April as a great day in the history of shipping, and they said this they gave utterance to a truth more awful than could be conceived by living man.

It was a great day also in the history of Southampton, for many fathers of families had found employment on the Titanic, many women's faces were lightened because the shadow of need and poverty had been banished from their homes.

It was a day that no one who stood upon the quayside will ever forget. We who saw it saw a sight that will be unforgettable until our eyes are turned to dust.

We saw the start of the mightiest vessel in the world upon her solitary and uncompleted voyage. She was named Titanic and she has been Titanic in her sorrow. We saw her, the mightiest, finest product of human brains in the matter of ships to sail the sea, a gigantic vessel that realised in her being a floating city of treasured glories, riches, and luxury, as she first ploughed the grey fields of the ocean.

And her displacement of water, the foam, and the rush of her passage, was so tremendous that the stern ropes of another mighty liner parted and the New York, but for the ready aid of holding tugs, would have swung out aimlessly into the fairway.

THE HAPPY START.

We paused in our cheering then, chilled to a sudden silence at this first evidence of the great ship's untested powers for evil as for good. And our cheering now is hushed into sobbing, for within a week of her majestic passage from Southampton Harbour, the displacement of the Titanic has been so tremendous that she has drenched the bosom of the world in an ocean of tears.

Those of us who had come to wish the vessel "Good speed"—in the dark wisdom of Providence to wish "God speed" and "a fair journey" to those loved ones who were going out upon the longest and loneliest voyage in Eternity—were up "by times" on that pleasant Wednesday morning, long before the stroke of noon when we knew Captain Smith would climb into his lofty perch on the navigating bridge and give the order to "let go" from the Trafalgar landing stage.

The air was busy with chatter, with "good bye for the present" and good wishes. We lived that morning in an atmosphere of pride. All these happy-faced Southampton women were proud that their men had entered into service on the greatest vessel ever built by man. They prattled of the Titanic with a sort of suggestion of proprietorship.

Rumours and legends and tales of her glories and luxuries and powers were bandied about in every street in Southampton. She was a caravanserai of marvels: a mighty treasure house of beauty and luxurious ease. In the phrase of the people, she was "the last word." The phrases of the people are often true, because they are double edged.

Another phrase sticks now in the puzzle of a darkening mind: "They're breaking all records this time." And so they were. It had been determined that the Titanic should excel in luxury and equipment her sister vessel, the Olympic, which had sailed for New York a week before. And in a sort of desperate endeavour to achieve this we who had come to take a temporary parting from dear ones and friends were shown a new and latest marvel on the promenade deck of the Titanic. It was called the Café Parisien. Its walls were covered with a delicate trellis work around which trailed cool foliage. We looked at the soft-cushioned chairs, we regarded the comfort of the whole scene, and, feeling the suggestive atmosphere of the place, thought of those who would be taking coffee there after dinner with music lulling every sense, melting into the gentle roll and rhythm of the open sea. What a place in which to dream!—perhaps if one were young to hold a little romantic dalliance—what a place in which to forget the trials and harass of the world! What a place in which to sleep!

Some of us looked into the private suites that were to cost a mere trifle of £870 a voyage, and here we found snug dining-rooms, bedrooms that looked in themselves like little enchanted palaces of slumberous rest, and private promenade decks. Let us note that everyone spoke of "dining-rooms" and "bedrooms." The word "cabin" would have been an anachronism in this floating citadel of luxurious beauty. We examined the delicate glass and napery, the flowers and the fruit, the baths and the playing-courts, and the innumerable mechanical appliances that seemed to make personal effort or discomfort the only human impossibility on board.

There was one thing that no one looking even for a brief half-hour on this cushioned lap of luxury ever thought of giving a cursory glance or a thought. No one looked at the boats.

Punctually at noon Captain E. J. Smith, a typical figure of an English sailor as we knew him and imagined him in tougher, pre-Titanic days, took up his post of captainship on the navigating bridge. And as the bells sounded, the cheers of the multitudes went upward and hands and handkerchiefs were waved from quay and ship's side, and kisses were blown across and last familiar greetings exchanged.

So she went away with her human freight of two thousand two hundred and eight souls. We cheered to the last and waved our salutations, and that night I think there was not an unhappy woman in all Southampton. And to-night—who is to count the tear-stained faces or to cast a reckoning over the travail of these broken hearts, some here, some two thousand miles away, but all united beyond the cleavage of the pitiless seas, by the sacred companionship of sorrow!

WHAT WE THOUGHT—

So the Titanic went her away, and we went ours, and thought perhaps little about her, save thoughts of remembered joy in her strength and beauty, until on Tuesday morning came the news that smote upon our hearts with the thunder of doom. These were, of course, the first indefinite rumblings that woke fear in every human breast.

She had struck an iceberg; she had been rent; but she was unsinkable. She was heading slowly for shore, a great giant wounded thing in the wake of the Virginian. How our hopes died down until it seemed that the heart was burnt into a heap of dead cold ashes, only to rise, Phœnix-like, in jubilant and hopeful expectancy. Human lips have sobbed out strange prayers before to-day, but what volume of prayer went up to heaven in thankfulness to the Lord of Hosts who had brought the new wonder of wireless telegraphy out of the slow womb of time.

We thought of that unforgettable message speeding through the viewless air that is marked upon the chart sheets S.O.S. We picked up the common phrase of the operator and repeated to ourselves: "Save Our Souls," and thanked Providence for their salvation.

We pictured the scene. The lonely operator, composed with that old English valiance that has turned the blood of history into wine, calmly tapping out the cry of help. We saw the realisation of that message in the operator's cabin on other vessels. We saw the wonderful chain composed of those three words, stronger than stone or iron or tempered steel, stronger than wind or sea, suddenly dragging all the vessels within the sphere of hearing away from their allotted course, and sending them on the great adventure of succour and mercy. We pictured them racing along the railless roads of the open sea, rushing with insensate speed towards the spot of the catastrophe. We had leisure to imagine the scene, because we were told there had been a great deliverance; because we felt that man had fought his battle with the ocean and had won.

Then we knew that we had lost.

—AND WHAT WE LEARNT.

All the world knows how slowly those confessions of defeat came in upon us, how slowly the last flicker of an expiring hope was beaten down within our breasts, with what dilatory hands the veils were drawn from the implacable face of doom. Gradually the hush laid hold upon us, gradually a realisation of what had happened sank into our souls.

We knew that nothing but a miserable residue of the great human freightage had been saved to us. We knew that the enchanted floating palace, conceived by the brain of man and wrought by his hands, with all its mighty scheme of luxurious ease, health, and comfort, lay somewhere tangled in an old sea forest, two miles beneath the quiet surface of the sea. Little more do we know as I write. We can only hear the sobbing of the women at the street corners of Southampton, and find in them an eternal echo of the cheers with which we sent the Titanic out on her first, her last, her only voyage.

We know that among these women are many mothers. We know with thankfulness that though their faces are dark with sorrow they are untouched with the lightest shadow of shame. For though man has been beaten once again in his old fight with the sea, yet he has done one thing with all the glory and splendour of a victory.

He has taken the last gift of God and used it well. He has died as we all would die—for others.

Picturing that last dark awful moment, the last order of the captain, the last farewells—so different from these we exchanged at Southampton—the last tears and the last high human courage, all our sorrow is tempered by the thought that the women are alive to us and the children, and that the men died as we would have had them die, as we should like to have died ourselves had God steeled our hearts with a similar courage.

Knowing this, as we peer into the dark picture of that yet unrecorded scene, so deep with human anguish and yet so lighted with human grandeur, we may learn to endure the sobbings of the women and the cries of the fatherless that come up to us in every surge of the immemorial sea. Knowing this, we may take comfort in the great cry of a great poet in a sea-washed island that had born so many poets, and acclaim with him that:—

Nothing is here for tears, nothing to wail,
Or knock the breast, no weakness, no contempt,
Dispraise or blame, nothing but well and fair,
And what may quiet us in a death so noble.

THE COMMANDER OF THE TITANIC AND THE BOWS OF HIS SHIP.

The portrait of Captain Smith was taken on board the Titanic on the day of the vessel's departure from Southampton. He was in command of the Olympic, the Titanic's sister ship, when, on her maiden voyage, she collided with H.M.S. Hawke.

THE DAILY GRAPHIC SPECIAL TITANIC IN MEMORIAM NUMBER, APRIL 20, 1912.

FEATURES WHICH CONTRIBUTED TO THE SPLENDOURS OF THE TITANIC.

A SINGLE BERTH STATE-ROOM.

A DECK STATE ROOM.

THE SWIMMING BATH, A POPULAR FEATURE WHICH IS POSSESSED BY VERY FEW VESSELS AFLOAT.

THE TURKISH BATH COOLING ROOM, WHICH, WITH ITS SUGGESTION OF THE "MYSTERIOUS EAST," IS ONE OF THE SHIP'S MOST INTERESTING ROOMS.

THE VERANDAH CAFE ADJOINING THE SMOKE ROOM. IT IS SURROUNDED BY GREEN TRELLIS-WORK, OVER WHICH GROW CLIMBING PLANTS.

THE MAIN STAIRCASE FROM THE GREAT HALL.—FROM THIS HALL LIFTS GO UP AND DOWN TO EVERY FLOOR OF THE SHIP.

In the 1912 world beyond South Wales, the *Titanic* had sunk with massive loss of life and there were slowly growing worries about the political relationships in the Balkans area of Eastern Europe where some smaller countries enjoyed the backing of more muscled-up political friends. Unsettling times.

Newspaper report about the Titanic by the Daily Graphic, April 20, 1912

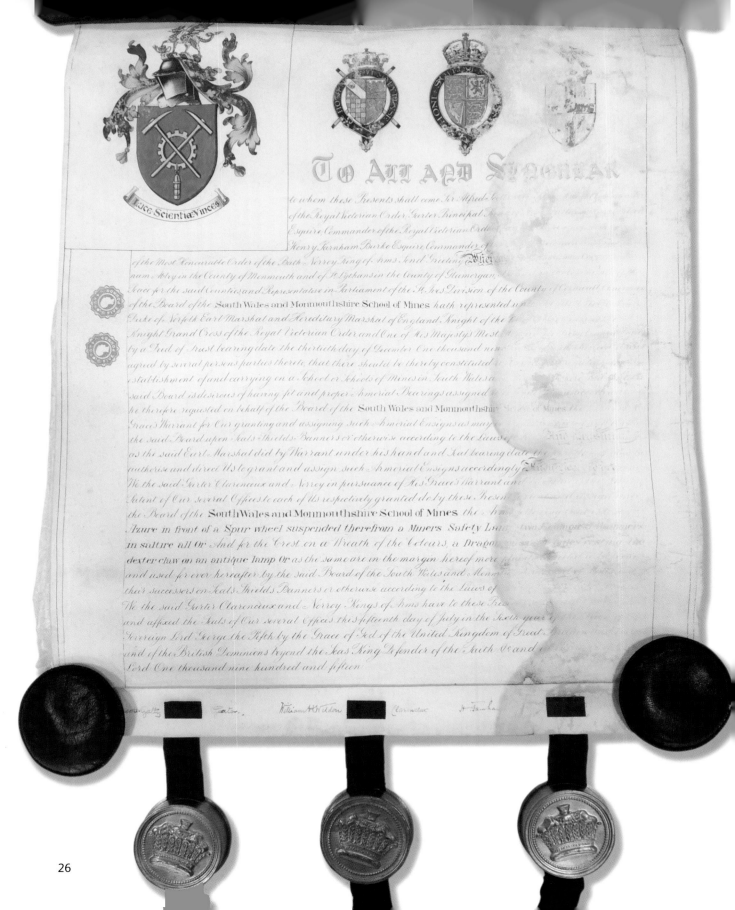

Faece Scientiæ Vinces

To All And Singular

...to whom these Presents shall come Sir Alfred...

...of the Royal Victorian Order Garter Principal...

...Esquire Commander of the Royal Victorian Order...

...Henry Farnham Burke Esquire Commander of...

...of the Most Honourable Order of the Bath Norroy King of Arms Send Greeting...

...nam Abbey in the County of Monmouth and of St Lythans in the County of Glamorgan...

...ace for the said Counties and Representative in Parliament of the St Ives Division of the County of Cornwall...

...of the Board of the South Wales and Monmouthshire School of Mines hath represented un...

...Duke of Norfolk Earl Marshal and Hereditary Marshal of England Knight of the...

...Knight Grand Cross of the Royal Victorian Order and One of His Majesty's Most...

...by a Deed of Trust bearing date the thirtieth day of December One thousand nine...

...agreed by several persons parties thereto that there should be thereby constituted...

...establishment of and carrying on a School or Schools of Mines in South Wales a...

...said Board is desirous of having fit and proper Armorial Bearings assigned...

...he therefore requested on behalf of the Board of the South Wales and Monmouthshire...

...Grace's Warrant for Our granting and assigning such Armorial Ensigns as may...

...the said Board upon Seals Shields Banners or otherwise according to the Laws...

...as the said Earl Marshal did by Warrant under his hand and Seal bearing date...

...authorise and direct Us to grant and assign such Armorial Ensigns accordingly...

...We the said Garter Clarenceux and Norroy in pursuance of His Grace's Warrant and...

...Patent of Our several Offices to each of Us respectively granted do by these Presents...

...the Board of the South Wales and Monmouthshire School of Mines the Arms...

...Azure in front of a Spur wheel suspended therefrom a Miners Safety Lamp two...

...in saltire all Or And for the Crest on a Wreath of the Colours, a Dragon...

...dexter claw on an antique lamp Or as the same are in the margin hereof more...

...and used for ever hereafter by the said Board of the South Wales and Monm...

...their successors on Seals Shields Banners or otherwise according to the Laws of...

...We the said Garter Clarenceux and Norroy Kings of Arms have to these Pre...

...and affixed the Seals of Our several Offices this fifteenth day of July in the Sixth year...

...Sovereign Lord George the Fifth by the Grace of God of the United Kingdom of Great...

...and of the British Dominions beyond the Seas King Defender of the Faith &c and...

...Lord One thousand nine hundred and fifteen.

In formal education around 1912, working class children had little hope or opportunity to reach an advanced level; even secondary education was something of an aspiration. It wasn't until the Fisher Education Act of 1918 that the school leaving age was raised from 12 years old and all fees for elementary education were abolished. Social mobility, the idea that free movement through social class is achievable as a result of one's talents and abilities rather than luck in one's parents, was way over a future horizon. An advanced education, such as that about to be offered by the South Wales and Monmouthshire School of Mines, was strictly for the fortunate. One knew one's place in 1912, and one generally stayed in it.

So, it might appear slightly anomalous that, at a time when the life of South Wales' colliers could be troubled, hungry and pretty much devoid of ambition, and when the still all-powerful coal owners were genuinely hated by the majority of working people for their hitherto exploitative attitudes, that discussions came to fruition for the establishment of a school for the advanced education of miners. And that the School should be funded from the profits of those same coal owners was equally remarkable; this was, after all, money that would otherwise have gone directly into their pockets.

Left: Despite some damage, the original document conferring the coat of arms of the South Wales and Monmouthshire School of Mines is still remarkably well preserved

The founders and their motivations

An event at the Deep Navigation Colliery, Treharris

Left to right:
E. M. Hann – Director of Powell Duffryn Steam Coal Company

Evan Williams – Chairman of Monmouthshire and South Wales Coal Owners Association

Hugh Bramwell – Director of the Great Western Colliery Co. Ltd.

W. North Lewis – Monmouthshire and South Wales Coal Owners Association, Insoles Colliery

Founding members of the South Wales and Monmouthshire School of Mines:

The Britannic Merthyr Coal Company Limited

Cambrian Collieries Limited

Cory Brothers Limited

David Davies and Sons Limited

Deep Navigation Collieries Limited

Insoles Limited

Naval Colliery Company Limited

Nixon's Navigation Limited

Powell Duffryn Steam Coal Company Limited

South Rhondda Colliery Company Limited

Ynyshir Steam Coal Company Limited

The founders of the South Wales and Monmouthshire School of Mines are often referred to as 'the Coal Owners', an adequate enough term as shorthand but one which is perhaps a little over-simple. 'Coal Owners' in this sense refers to the men or companies who owned the coal mines and dominated the industry in those days before the National Coal Board came into being.

This particular group was formally known as the *Monmouthshire and South Wales Coal-Owners' Association* and, by 1908/09, a number of important members were expressing their opinion that a pool of qualified men was needed from which they could draw their colliery officials. This was because the industry generally had seen enormous growth and this coalfield in particular was shortly to reach its peak of production, something which was accompanied with a growing government emphasis on safety in the industry. And so the idea grew, with the major movers and shakers being names which are well recognised in the industrial history of South Wales, many of which are still reflected in local place names, street names or buildings.

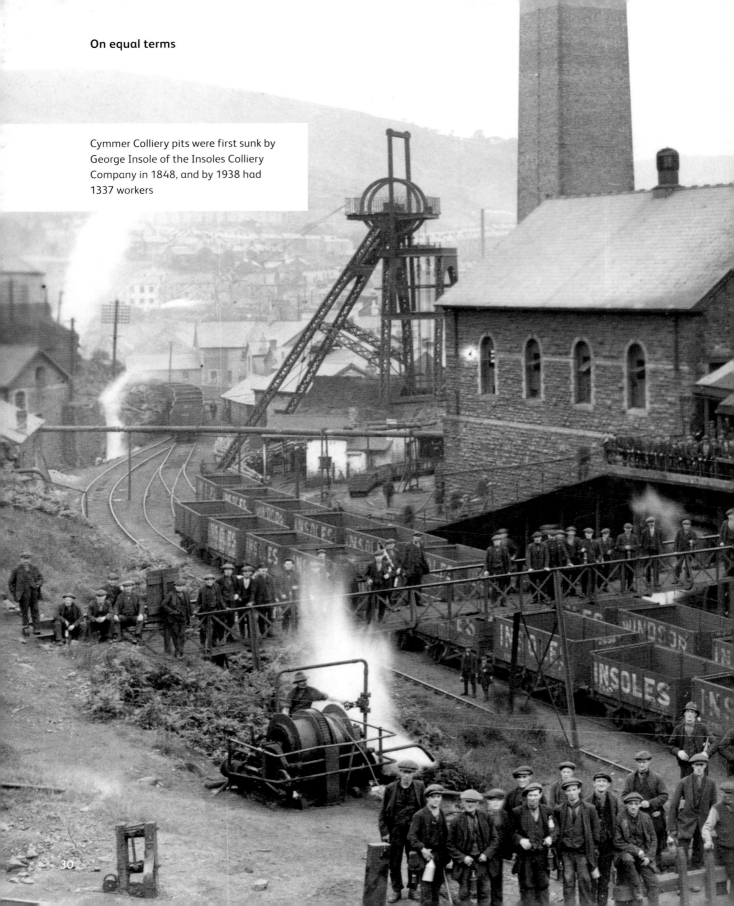

On equal terms

Cymmer Colliery pits were first sunk by George Insole of the Insoles Colliery Company in 1848, and by 1938 had 1337 workers

'2,400 tons had to be produced to raise just £1 of funds for the School.'

By 4th November 1912 the Coal Owners' Association had received 'approval slips' from the representatives of these 11 companies to a proposal that a school be established for the advanced education of miners. Furthermore it was accepted that the School be funded from a levy attached to every ton of coal produced from the collieries of the 11 companies. The enlightened Mr Samuel Rogers would have been delighted.

The proposal was that the School should be funded by a levy of 1/10 of a pre-decimal penny applied to every ton of coal produced. From a modern perspective this seems such a small amount, and it meant that 2,400 tons had to be produced to raise just £1 of funds for the School. But it is hard for us, 100 years later and with the merest shadow of a coal industry remaining, to get any sense of the scale of the

Above: Ynyshir Colliery

Top right: Coed Ely, Colliery

Right: Cambrian Collieries

COED ELY, TONYREFAIL

Cambrian Collieries, Clydach Vale

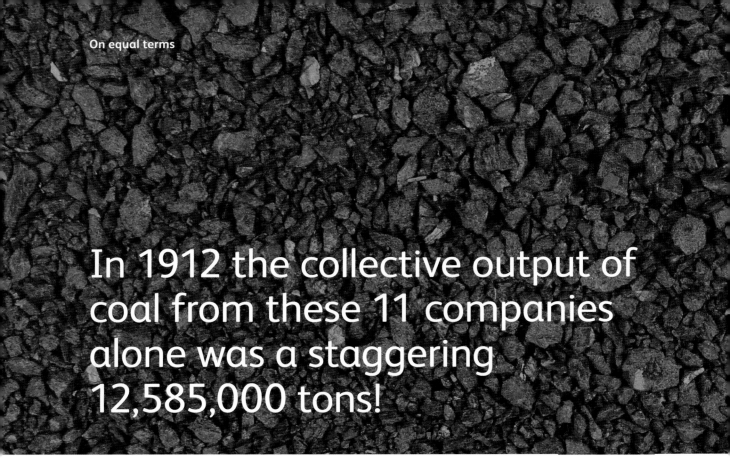

In 1912 the collective output of coal from these 11 companies alone was a staggering 12,585,000 tons!

industry at that time and therefore for the lavish funding that this modest levy actually produced. In 1912 the collective output of coal from these 11 companies alone was a staggering 12,585,000 tons! So applying a little arithmetic: that's 1,258,500 pennies or £5,243.15s. It still doesn't sound like a fortune, but think of it like this: in 1913 a young, ordinary hewer of coal (the collier who might dearly wish to be sent to the School of Mines) would earn around 10/6 per week. In that context the £5,243.15s of 1913 is worth approximately half a million pounds at 2012 values, and it was certainly an abundant budget to start off the new venture. In later years, more member companies of the Coal Owners' Association agreed that the levy could be applied to their output and so this generous budget increased nicely as the School became established and respected.

You might imagine that an existing provider of advanced education such as the University College of South Wales and Monmouthshire in Cardiff (est. 1883) would very much welcome that level of investment. It might have expanded and developed the already well-established and reputable mining department which had been led by the eminent Professor (later Sir) William Galloway. But the investment clearly did not go in that direction or the University of Glamorgan would not be celebrating its centenary in 2013. A separate, independent school was set up and this seemingly idiosyncratic decision needs some explanation as it was to remain a contentious issue for many years.

Top right: Gelli Colliery

Right: Penygraig & Tonypandy, showing Penygraig Naval Colliery

8052 GELLI COLLIERY YSTRA

GENERAL VIEW of PENYGRAIG & TONYPANDY. 726

Cardiff
or Treforest?

A number of writers have debated
the reasons behind the Coal Owners'
decision to establish a separate School
of Mines, independent of the University
College in Cardiff. Theories tend to
centre on the design of the curriculum
and the structure and governance of the
University itself.

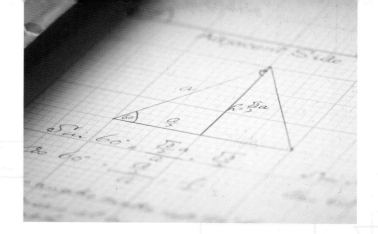

The curriculum

There's no doubt that, for the Coal Owners, the curriculum at Cardiff was a major stumbling block to investing at the University. A luminary of the School of Mines, Mr Hugh Ingledew (the Secretary of the original Mining Board which managed the School) wrote in a booklet celebrating the School's 21st birthday in 1934 that '...it was found that the limitations of the Charter of the University College did not permit the establishment on a joint scientific and technical basis of a sandwich system of education ...'. What that means is that the University wanted to teach 'pure science', but the Coal Owners needed men to get a mixture of science and a good technical, engineering education applied to the coal industry. The Coal Owners also wanted a 'sandwich' education in which the students spent time applying classroom knowledge in a hands-on way in the workplace. But the University wouldn't allow this kind of interference in its curriculum and it resisted this now familiar format until into the mid 1920s. All of which seems pretty strange from today's twenty-first century perspective! But in 1934 Mr Ingledew was probably being somewhat diplomatic in his choice of words since

'the Coal Owners needed men to get a mixture of science and a good technical, engineering education applied to the coal industry.'

the Coal Owners' decision was, even then, still being revisited in discussions, meetings and arguments, and some tensions continued to drag on until the early years of World War II.

There is, of course, always a bigger picture, one which incorporates more than just the University's inability or unwillingness to use a sandwich system of education. It's much more likely that, whilst this was a major reason for the establishment of a separate school, it was not the only one. There are other pretty compelling reasons which, when taken together, suggest that Treforest was a sensible choice all round.

The facilities

One sound reason for investing in a new facility at Treforest was that the University College did not have established buildings of good enough quality capable of educating the numbers of men the coal companies wanted.

In those days the University was located in its original spot in the old Infirmary building on Newport Road and the main building was supplemented by what was described as 'a series of ramshackle huts'. Because of woeful overcrowding, students in the Mining and Geology department were actually taught in the house of Professor Galloway, who was no longer employed by the University but who rented his former home as classrooms for £15 per year! Thinking about the Coal Owners' position, they must have given consideration to the amount of time and effort which would be needed to turn this dilapidated department into a cutting edge teaching environment, even with the considerable purchasing power at their disposal. It's also likely that the speed of movement of the Senate and its decision making machinery just wouldn't fit with the dynamism of the coal industry leaders, a group who were more familiar with a 'do-it-and-do-it-now' approach to management.

Above: Treforest 1909 shortly before the establishment of the school

Greek and Latin
in the mining industry?

Related to the (not) fit-for-purpose nature of the curriculum at the University, it also seems likely that Coal Owners such as entrepreneurial liberal Sir Clifford Cory and David Thomas (later to be Lord Rhondda) also took into account some peripheral but no less difficult issues such as the University's requirement that mining students should have a knowledge of Greek and Latin! (In fact, this requirement on the part of the University continued on for another 10 years, only coming to an end in 1923). To be fair, this is more of a reflection on the nature of higher education at the time, but putting yourself in the mind of David Hannah of the Cambrian Group, it's hard to see how this could be considered a sensible use of your men's time. And bearing in mind the state of secondary education and its inaccessibility to working class men, how likely would the Coal Owners be to find men in their workforce who already had the knowledge of Greek and Latin the University wanted?

Above: In his youth, Sir Clifford Cory was once described as one of the 'rising young coal kings of South Wales...'

Funding
not managing

The Coal Owners in 1912 were preparing to spend a vast sum of money on miners' education. Generally speaking, in early twentieth-century education circles, this alone would have provided any benefactor with a place on a board of management where his views would have been respectfully considered. In short, money talked. In this instance, from the Coal Owners point of view, it would have been about more than just status. It would have been essential for the industry leaders to at least have a say in the departments, courses or choice of teachers they were paying for. It's doubtful that a seat on the Senate was ever really expected, and no management place of any sort was offered. In fact, the very opposite seems to have been true with clear hostility being shown by the Senate towards the Coal Owners. But as the School began to flourish, neither the School's Principal, Professor George Knox, nor Sir Clifford Cory for the Coal Owners, held back in their criticisms of the University College and its management. When speaking to the Haldane Commission (a First World War period investigation into university level education in South Wales) Professor Knox described the University's BSc course as serving no useful purpose 'so far as our coalfield is concerned.' In the same vein Sir Clifford Cory also told the Commission that 'the Mining Department of the [University] College...had entirely failed to provide the class of instruction which the Coal Owners required for the purposes of their business'.

Britannic Colliery

41

The School of Mines, Crumlin.

Geography of the coalfield

When the School of Mines was planned in the early years of the twentieth century, the plans didn't include any residential courses and so there were no halls of residence or similar. All of the students were going to be men who lived and worked in the area. Some would be studying on a full-time basis but they would be living at home and working for weeks at a time in the coalfield. However, many more students were going to be working full-time and studying part-time; either coming along to the School after a day's work or being given day release to attend for one full day a week. It wouldn't have been impossible for these students to travel by public transport to Newport Road in Cardiff for their tuition, although this would have been something of a bind after 10 or 12 hours in a colliery! But it would have been a lot easier to get to Treforest, which was surrounded by extremely convenient rail links from many of the valleys.

Treforest was enormously well placed to serve the coalfield, a fact noted in the 1927 report of the Board of Education's inspection of the School which declared 'Treforest...is easily approached by rail from the large mining areas in the valleys of the Taff, Rhondda, Cynon, Rhymney, and their tributaries'. The second campus of the School of Mines, which opened a year later at Crumlin in Monmouthshire, was equally well placed to serve the eastern valleys of the coalfield. A third campus, planned in extensive detail, was to be opened at Swansea to serve the western coalfield, but this plan was scuppered by the declaration of war in August 1914, and never resurrected. The careful thought around these three locations shows that geography must have been a factor in the final decision; possibly not the key issue but certainly one of importance. It wouldn't have been too difficult, of course, for the University College to manage a 'campus' in Treforest, and perhaps this was always going to be the location whoever was responsible for running it. However, the extent to which the Senate was prepared and willing to manage a satellite campus close to the valleys is clearly open to question.

Top left: Crumlin Campus in 1914

Left: Davey Lamp made by E Thomas & Williams, Cambrian Lamp Works, Aberdare

Right: 1912 map of the Barry Railway: a section of which is now the Treforest Campus

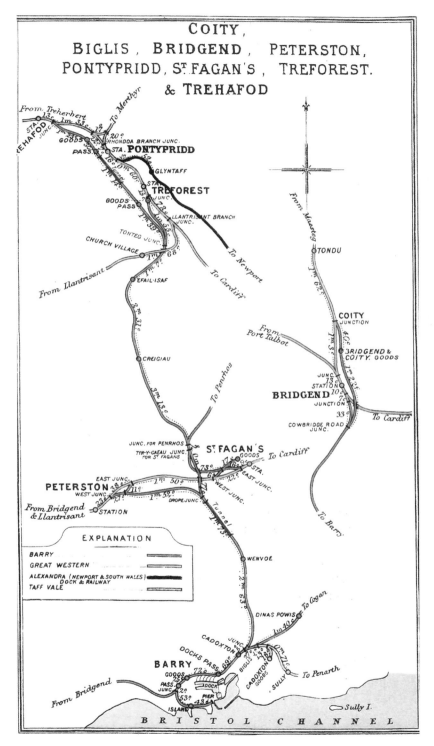

A convenient building

The obvious commodity needed if one is contemplating setting up a school is a building of the right size and calibre. The University College in Cardiff didn't have one, as already noted, so presumably that would have necessitated the construction of a new building or the acquisition and conversion of an existing building – if, that is, something happened to be available at the time. The Barry Railway Company did have a building of the right size and of suitable status: Forest House, formerly home of the 'Iron Prince' Francis Crawshay and,

later, of Walter Morgan, a well known local solicitor. It's extremely interesting to ponder why, if 'serious' negotiations were still in hand with the University College up to and beyond 1912, the Coal Owners had already gone ahead and obtained the house with no input to this decision from the Senate. The Barry Railway Company had bought tracts of land in Treforest in order to build their line to the new Barry Docks and the company had also bought the house and the adjacent large field in 1912 from the widow of Walter Morgan.

Above: Forest House

Right: Barry Docks at the culmination of the Barry Railway line

Entrance to New Dock, Hydraulic Bridge, Barry Dock

And, significantly, there was considerable overlap in the membership of the management group of Barry Railway Company and the Coal Owners' Association...who had need of a building! The ownership of the house is one more piece in the jigsaw of reasons why Treforest and not Cardiff became the site of the South Wales and Monmouthshire School of Mines.

It's difficult for us to imagine just how different and unconventional this action of the Coal Owners was at the time. In the twenty-first century we are entirely familiar with tailoring a curriculum to meet the needs of employers and almost all universities and colleges would welcome the opportunity to co-develop courses and resources with industrial leaders. It would now be a cause for a major celebration! Yet for all the reasons given above the decision was made – it was to be Treforest, and independence!

'The ownership of the house is one more piece in the jigsaw of reasons why Treforest and not Cardiff became the site of the South Wales and Monmouthshire School of Mines.'

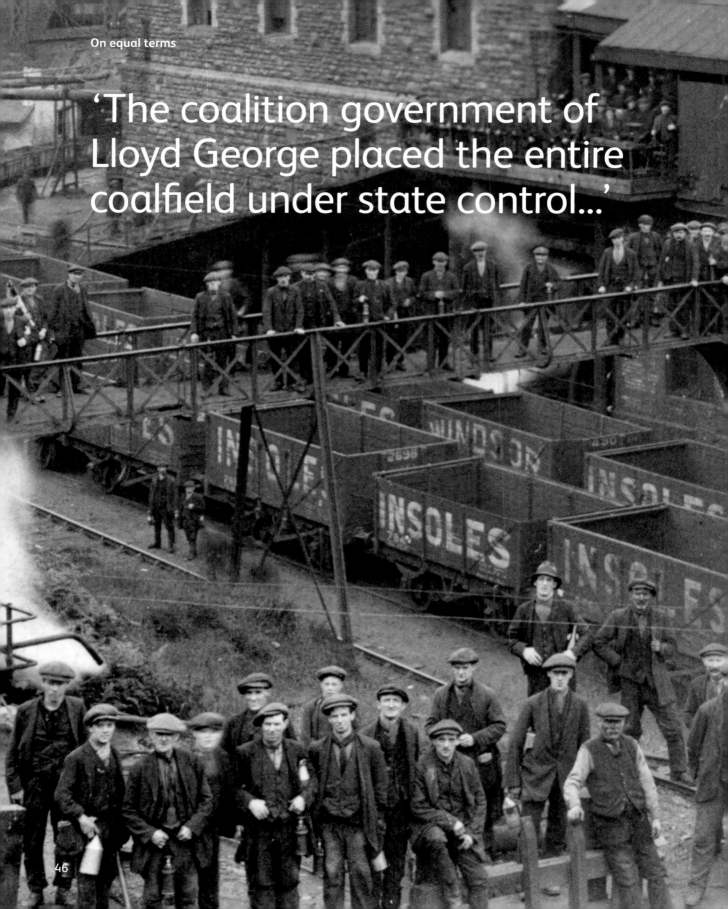

'The coalition government of Lloyd George placed the entire coalfield under state control...'

However, it still wasn't the end of the matter as the (then) Glamorgan County Council continued to wring its collective hands, hold committee meetings and write reports about why the Coal Owners did what they did. They aired new concerns that this cheeky junior institution may be able to tap into mainstream funds for its courses. In one such confidential report dated January 1916 the clerk to the council wrote that "if their [the Coal Owners] present Napoleonic fight should succeed by receiving government grants in aid, then there will be even greater industrial troubles in this important coalfield". A clear implication that the School of Mines ought not receive money from the public purse and a vision of serious trouble to come if it did.

The reference to 'troubles' alludes to the extremely difficult decades of the early twentieth century in the South Wales coalfield: only months before this confidential report was written 200,000 miners had been on strike despite the clear demand at the time for coal production to aid the war effort.

The coalition government of Lloyd George placed the entire coalfield under state control shortly after, so the County Council was certainly not the only body to be concerned about 'troubles'. However, the terminology used in this report is very emotive and reveals the depth of feelings that existed about this controversial decision of the Coal Owners' Association.

Establishing the School!

Did the Monmouthshire and South Wales Coal Owners' Association have a point to prove once their decision to go independent was made? It certainly did! The Coal Owners would clearly have needed to protect their reputation and prestige, not to mention their significant investment, and this School just had to work, and work very well indeed. To fail at this point would have resulted in more than just the failure of a place of learning; the credibility of the Coal Owners was at stake.

So it's worth taking a moment to think about what happened next. How would a new university-level institution be put together today? There would be a steering group chaired by an experienced VIP. There would be different tasks being managed and rolled out through specialist sub committees – marketing, building, procurement, curriculum design and validation. As a scenario it's all pretty familiar and entirely proper. However, in the foreign country of 1912 things were a bit different.

Against
the clock

The School was placed under the management and control of a 'Mining Board' which consisted of representatives, two each, from the subscribing collieries and chaired, unsurprisingly, by Sir Clifford Cory of Cory Brothers & Company Ltd. In the summer of 1913 the Board was preparing for the opening of the School and membership had expanded from the original 11 companies which agreed to set up the School to 14 companies (with consequent, welcome increases in the budget for the School). The later additions were the Glamorgan Coal Company Ltd, the Ocean Coal Company Ltd, and the Penrikyber Navigation Colliery Company Ltd, with numerous other companies set to join as subscribers as the early years went on. The Secretary to the Board was the eminent Cardiff solicitor, Hugh Ingledew, an extremely well known and respected Oxford University graduate who had been a Welsh international rugby union forward, playing for Cardiff RFC and winning three caps for Wales and another for the Barbarians. He was a man of many parts, he also played cricket for Glamorgan.

The Board decided that a 'Director of Mining' should be sought – this was the formal title of the Principal of the School – and Hugh Ingledew, writing in 1934, tells us that the Board instructed that the Director should be the "the very best man obtainable". Generally, when the very best is chosen it is an expensive business and this makes clear that the Coal Owners were backing up their plans with the resources needed to bring them to a successful launch.

The advertisement for the Director was placed on the 17th January 1913, Professor George Knox was appointed. Joining him on the small team of teaching staff were:

1. John Samuel – Assistant Director of Mining (front row)

2. Fred H. Downie – Senior Lecturer in Electrical Engineering

3. Edgar C. Evans – Senior Lecturer in Chemistry (front row)

4. Robert (Bobby) James – Senior Lecturer in Mechanical Engineering (front row)

5. Richard Richards – Assistant Lecturer in Mining and Geology.

C. K. DAVIES.   J. C. PRICE.   R. ISAAC.   A. REYNOLDS.   D. JOHN.   E. E. EVANS.

R. LAWRENCE.   A. BUNDY.   P. S. H. JONES.   T. C. LEWIS.   W. E. PRIDE.   I. POWELL.   D. WILLIAMS.   W. KNOX.   W. S. JONES.

MR. BOWMAN.   G. THOMAS.   M. LEWIS.   D. W. GRIFFITHS.   J. DAVIES.   D. J. HOWELLS.   J. S. JERMAINE.   BLACKWELL JONES.   MR. J. H. ROBERTS.

MR. E. EVANS.   MR. W. T. LANE.   MR. R. M. METCALF.   DR. S. ROY ILLINGWORTH.   PROFESSOR G. KNOX.   MR. J. SAMUEL.   MR. R. JAMES.   MR. W. W. FIRTH.   MR. J. BRIGHAM.

This is the teaching team which had around nine months, January to October 1913, to put together a fully functioning School of Mines. Although sadly now invisible in the records, there must have been a small team of secretarial, administrative and technical staff who worked with the teaching staff to bring off a remarkable achievement in the time available. They completed the conversion of the house, purchased and installed state-of-the-art equipment, designed the curriculum, the timetable and the assessments, and liaised with the coal companies over which students would be the first through the doors. Thinking through the logistics of this herculean task, it seems extremely likely that some of the preparatory work was in hand or, at the very least, planned before those all-important approval slips were received from the Coal Owners. Even so, it has to be said that the achievement is truly astonishing.

Above: Staff and final year students 1924-25

Tŷ Crawshay

Treforest is a small place but by around 1836 it was home to probably the largest tinplate works in the world and it was in the ownership of the famous Crawshay Family. The Treforest works was under the control of Francis Crawshay and he and his family lived in the suitably grand Forest House from around 1831. Francis himself was a very interesting character, not entirely business-like at times, and his story would make great reading but is perhaps better suited to another occasion.

By the early twentieth century his former home was still largely in its original shape, being comprised of two storeys, gardens, adjacent workers' cottages and the usual outbuildings associated with a large house. On the north side of the house was a good-sized field, more or less where the University's current Brecon and Cynon buildings now stand, and at the furthest end of this Francis had erected a circle of standing stones and its centre stone commemorated many members of his family'. This small estate was the 'raw material' which would become the School of Mines.

As it was, the house wasn't large enough to accommodate modern laboratories and teaching rooms, and the ceiling and floor joists would almost certainly have been at risk if heavy industrial machinery were installed. So a two-storey annexe was added to the south side of the house, complete with an attractive castellated roof line and

Above: Illustration of Tŷ Crawshay by staff member R.M. Metcalfe

Left: Tŷ Crawshay today

51

On equal terms

Right: Various pieces of mining machinery such as the Gutermuth pump were used to educate students at the School

Below: Text books gave students detailed information regarding mining equipment, structure and practices. In this example a page from 'Practical Coal-mining' shows mine shaft mechanisms and structure

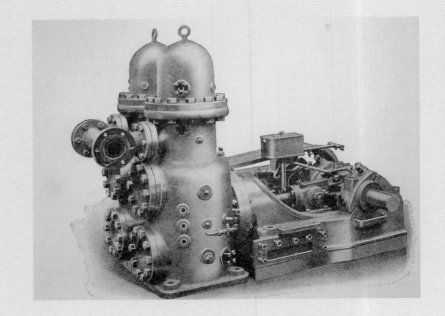

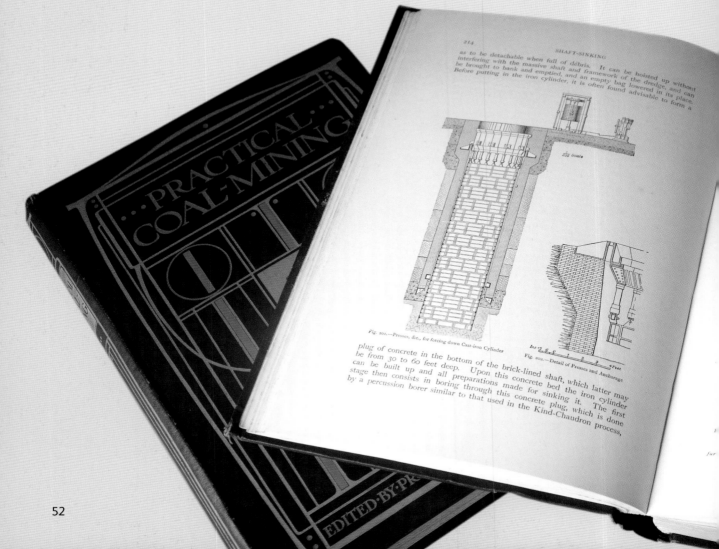

PRACTICAL COAL-MINING

EDITED BY PR...

214

SHAFT-SINKING

as to be detachable when full of débris. It can be hoisted up without interfering with the massive shaft and framework of the dredge, and can be brought to bank and emptied, and an empty bag lowered in its place. Before putting in the iron cylinder, it is often found advisable to form a

Fig. 201.—Presses, &c., for forcing down Cast-iron Cylinder

Fig. 202.—Detail of Presses and Anchorage

plug of concrete in the bottom of the brick-lined shaft, which latter may be from 30 to 60 feet deep. Upon this concrete bed the iron cylinder can be built up and all preparations made for sinking it. The first stage then consists in boring through this concrete plug, which is done by a percussion borer similar to that used in the Kind-Chaudron process, gothic style large windows to make use of the available light. Into this building went workshops for electrical and mechanical engineering on the ground floor; the heavy stuff. On the first floor were well equipped laboratories for gas testing, and for geology, chemistry, physics and mining. The old house itself was adapted by eminent Cardiff architects, Teather and Wilson (who had designed the opulent Baltic House in Cardiff Bay), to include lecture rooms, a students' common room, Professor Knox's office, the board room and students' cloak rooms, as well as a museum in the original hallway. On the first floor the old house contained lecture rooms to match the adjacent subject laboratories in the new wing and there were two large drawing offices in the rooms overlooking the front steps. And beneath the new wing was a massive water tank which probably had a dual purpose: to enable students to be taught pumping and mine safety techniques and to drive the water turbine known to be at the School in 1913 and which may well have contributed to the power supply for the workshops.

The oily wrapping was probably still on the machinery and the smell of paint all pervasive when the students arrived.

Below: Theodolite used in mine surveying for measuring angles in the horizontal and vertical planes

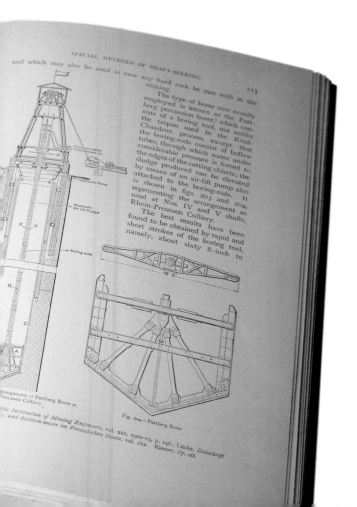

The first curriculum

It just has to be the case that the experienced (and expensive!) staff who were appointed to put together the first curriculum and teach it, brought with them the curriculum or ideas they had been teaching at their previous place of employment. This is not to be considered unethical, instead it is perfectly sensible. There was no direct competition between, for example, the Wigan Mining and Technical College (Professor Knox's previous employer) and the South Wales and Monmouthshire School of Mines. Students simply didn't look at the range of colleges offering mining education and choose where to go as they do in the twenty-first century; they went to college locally and where their employers sent them. The detail of the curriculum would have been quickly designed or adapted to make it applicable to the South Wales coal field; taking account of matters such as local geology, the tendencies for the presence of gas and water, the way coal was moved from colliery to port, the placing of colliery waste, and so on. Even with their previous experience, it was a considerable task to get the courses ready for the first, new term of the 1913-14 academic year.

The School of Mines prospectus of 1913 shows that there were six original courses: a 3-year full-time mining course of 30 hours a week; 4-year part-time day courses of 8 hours a week each designed for Mine Managers, Mechanics, Electricians and Chemists and a 3-year part-time course (again of one 8 hour day) for Mine Surveyors.

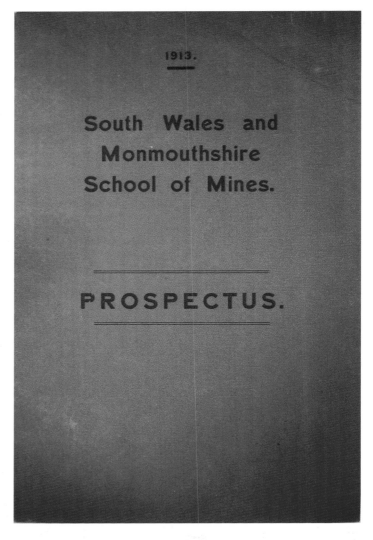

1913.

South Wales and Monmouthshire School of Mines.

PROSPECTUS.

As the Coal Owners had always wanted, the full-time course mixed classroom-based study with at least four months practical experience in the mine during the summer. During these months the students kept a diary which was signed off or approved by the Colliery Manager where they were employed; today this type of written account is still used and of value in many subjects; often assessed, as was the case in 1913, with an employer and academic tutor working in conjunction.

The classroom-based elements of the courses ran with what looks like the best of engineering precision. It is possible to look back and accurately picture what the students were studying, in exactly which rooms they were at certain times of the week, and even when they took their lunch break. The teaching day started at 9.00 am (yes, including Mondays), and finished promptly at 4.00 pm with the structure the same every day; teaching in two-hour blocks and no concession for extra-curricular activities such as sports matches on Wednesday afternoons! This means the full-time students had a teaching week of 30 hours class-contact time, although it's fair to point out that this must have included a good amount of workshop instruction, rather than just formal lectures.

The students who enrolled on the part-time courses were, of course, already employed in the coal field and their own work 'placements' were therefore ready-made. The part-time students were all employees of the subscribing colliery companies, although non-subscribing companies could send their own men along for a higher fee.

The sandwich system of mixing academic and theoretical learning with application in the work-place was, and still is, a model which works extremely well, especially for vocational courses which have a strong focus on employment experiences. It's interesting to note that the University College refused to embrace this format for at least another ten years – and probably changed the landscape of South Wales advanced education as a result.

The very first prospectus of the School of Mines is a gem of its type and within it, after the glorious architectural elevations and floor plans and self-confident lists of the teaching staff, are a couple of paragraphs about the *Objects of the School*. It's gently assertive about the benefits of the partnership with industry, and it's proud of the facilities and equipment on offer. Yet the very best bit, the bit which has always sat comfortably on this institution's shoulders, is where it says that, after allowing for academic ability, *'the School is open to all students on equal terms...'*. Which was not exactly the normal way of things for University level learning in 1913.

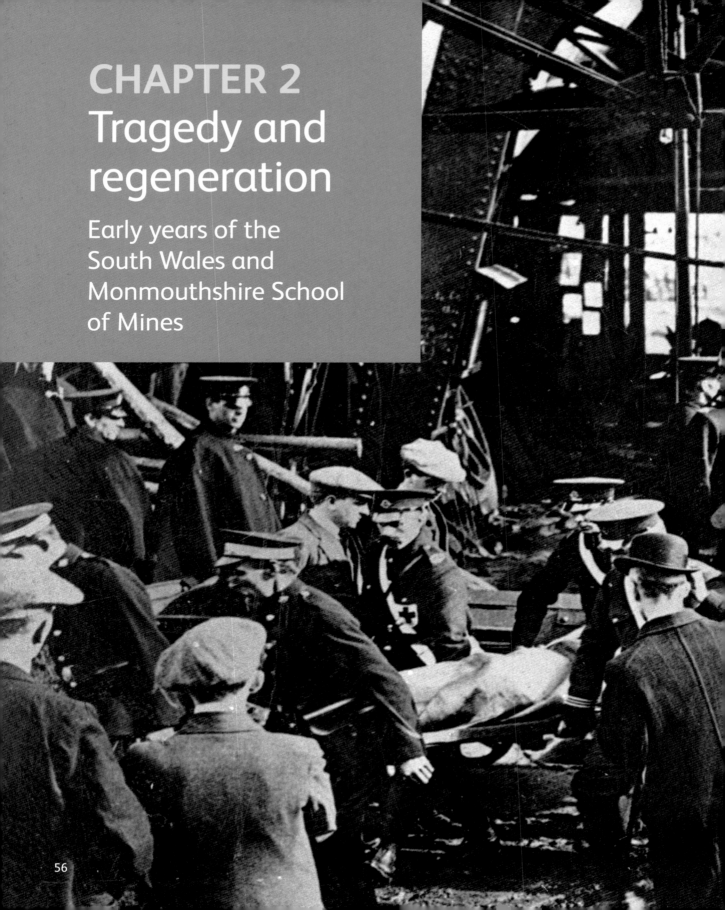

CHAPTER 2
Tragedy and regeneration

Early years of the
South Wales and
Monmouthshire School
of Mines

Welsh Pit Disaster. A little mother waiting for news.

Benton.
138 George St
Glasgow. 18.

Having argued, persuaded, and politicked their way through the early twentieth-century, by 1913 the Coal Owners' Association might have expected that they, the School of Mines and the staff team, could now concentrate on the real business of education. Not so.

To describe the national political picture in 1913 as 'tense' would be to seriously understate things, and the situation in South Wales' coalfield society was no different. You wouldn't need to be a learned person or a high level politician to see that, by the time the School of Mines opened its doors to its first students on October 8th 1913, society was seriously edgy about the likelihood of war. You wouldn't need to be a leading light in the 'Fed' or involved in miners' welfare groups to know that the

industry was still enormously troubled, not to mention dangerous to the health and well-being of its community. To put things bluntly, if you were aiming to pick an auspicious time to launch a new place of learning, then you got it wrong, big time, in choosing 1913. But of course 1913 wasn't chosen as such, it was simply the time at which the necessary agreements came together, the Coal Mines Act of 1911 re-set the priority on safety in mining, and the desire existed in the coalfield to establish a School. However, many of these tensions would have touched the School, of that there can be no doubt.

In South Wales, just as anxieties about peace or war were building, the coal industry threw in a few tensions of its own. Building on the lockout of striking miners in 1910 and the subsequent

Above: A mother and her child looking on as miners and their families react to the devastating explosion at the Universal Colliery at Senghenydd October 1913

'...straight over the mountain opposite the School, the Universal Colliery at Senghenydd exploded killing 439 men and boys.'

riots in Tonypandy (a series of actions which involved some 12,000 men), between February and April 1912 the industry's people suffered through a 37-day National Coal Strike which, at its peak, involved nearly a million workers. The strike sought to establish some consistency in wages so as to even-out local unfairness, as well as to secure a minimum wage. The Minimum Wage Act of 1912 was largely the solution and brought peace of a sort. However, for South Wales the worst was yet to come.

Just six days after the School of Mines opened its doors for the first time, about three miles away, straight over the mountain opposite the School, the Universal Colliery at Senghenydd exploded, killing 439 men and boys. The initial blast – to be followed by a series of fires as the coal dust and methane ignited – was so violent that it blew the two-ton cage (the lift for transporting coal and men) up and out of the Lancaster shaft and jammed it into the pit head winding gear above. Did the staff and students in Treforest hear the explosions that Tuesday morning as they came into School? We can't know. But as working colliers with daily concerns about safety, what would be the mood amongst the community of the School of Mines in those days and weeks? What would be the feelings and concerns of both staff and students?

'With this scale of disaster on the local doorstep it's hard to imagine that people's thoughts turned to the likelihood of war.'

Senghenydd turned out to be the most deadly mining disaster in British history with an estimated 1,000 people in the area bereaved as a consequence. This monstrous crime went on to cause even greater bitterness in the coalfield when the results of the official enquiry became known. It found that many responsibilities could be laid at the door of the owners and managers but when compensation and fines were meted out, they amounted to just £24. As one local newspaper calculated, that's just over a shilling for every life. On a slightly more positive note, the School of Mines, even in its first days, was able to offer valuable expertise as its staff worked on a solution to quench the underground fire at the Senghenydd Colliery which followed the explosion.

With this scale of disaster on the local doorstep it's hard to imagine that people's thoughts turned to the likelihood of war. But by 1913 the road to war was arguably already clear as a number of significant international incidents followed one another, making a major European war inevitable. This series of events culminated in the assassination of Archduke Franz Ferdinand of Austria, heir to the Austro-Hungarian throne, in the summer of 1914, an act which caused the system of alliances between the European nations to come into play and brought about a domino effect of country after country declaring themselves to be at war.

The effects of war on the coal industry would be immense and this would have been in the minds of the Coal Owners and discussed at every board, including the Board of Management of the School of Mines. The importance of the industry to the war effort was reflected by the Government's takeover of the coal mines under the Defence of the Realm Act in 1914.

Right: Postcards depicting the locality and aftermath of the Senghenydd Mine disaster in October 1913

Welsh Pit Disaster. A Street in Senghenydd. A Victim in every house.

The Great Welsh disaster at Senghenydd. Removing some of the Victims.

The first day of the first term,
first students and first staff

How special must it have felt to be in the first ever class at the new institution? So exciting, so full of optimism, a little trepidation... new experiences and new friends to be made!

Admission to the new School of Mines was not through any system of patronage, or by being favoured by a colliery manager. Advertisements describing the School and its courses were placed in the *Western Mail*, *Pontypridd Observer*, the *Echo* and the *Newport Argus*. Applicants for places on the full-time day mining courses then sat entrance examinations which were held at 10.00 a.m. on Tuesday, 23rd September 1913.

The results were announced the following week and, if a candidate had done well enough, he was offered a place. Part-time students had to be over 16 years of age and, as the 1913 prospectus helpfully informs its readers, have

"sufficient practical experience and elementary technical knowledge of the branch of mining covered by the course for which they wish to enrol".

Left: South Wales and Monmouthshire School of Mines seal

Right: Provisional timetable showing 'day mining course' taken from the first prospectus 1913

PROVISIONAL TIME TABLE—DAY MINING COURSE.

Subject.	Monday.	Tuesday.	Wednesday	Thursday.	Friday.
FIRST YEAR—					
Mathematics	9-11	—	—	9-11	—
Chemistry	11-1	—	9-11	—	9 11
Engineering Drawing	—	9-11	—	—	—
Surveying I.	—	11-1	—	—	11-1
Mechanics	—	—	11-1	11-1	—
Physics	—	2-4	—	—	2-4
Geology	—	—	2-4	2-4	—
Colliery Practice	2-4	—	—	—	—

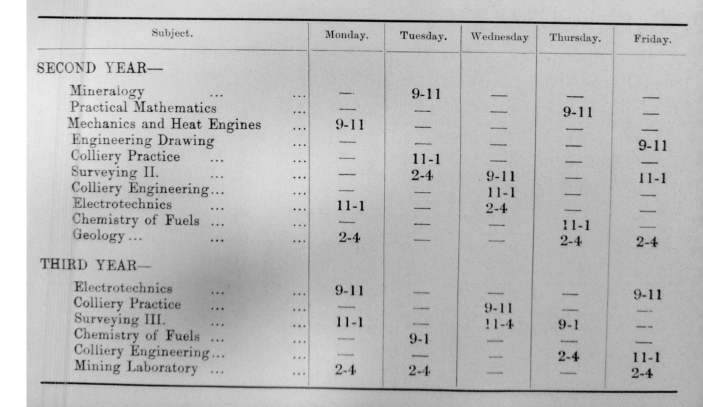

Subject.	Monday.	Tuesday.	Wednesday	Thursday.	Friday.
SECOND YEAR—					
Mineralogy	—	9-11	—	—	—
Practical Mathematics	—	—	—	9-11	—
Mechanics and Heat Engines	9-11	—	—	—	—
Engineering Drawing	—	—	—	—	9-11
Colliery Practice	—	11-1	—	—	—
Surveying II.	—	2-4	9-11	—	11-1
Colliery Engineering	—	—	11-1	—	—
Electrotechnics	11-1	—	2-4	—	—
Chemistry of Fuels	—	—	—	11-1	—
Geology	2-4	—	—	2-4	2-4
THIRD YEAR—					
Electrotechnics	9-11	—	—	—	9-11
Colliery Practice	—	—	9-11	—	—
Surveying III.	11-1	—	11-4	9-1	—
Chemistry of Fuels	—	9-1	—	—	—
Colliery Engineering	—	—	—	2-4	11-1
Mining Laboratory	2-4	2-4	—	—	2-4

PROVISIONAL TIME TABLES.

COLLIERY MANAGERS' COURSE.

Year.	Day.	9-11.	11-1.	2-4.	4-6.
1st	Monday	Mechanics and Heat Engines	Chemistry of Fuels	Colliery Practice I.	Practical Mathematics
2nd	Tuesday	Mechanics and Heat Engines	Surveying I.	Colliery Practice II.	Practical Mathematics
3rd	Wednes.	Surveying II.	Colliery Practice III.	Electrotechnics I.	Geology I.
4th	Thursday	Electrotechnics II.	Surveying III.	Colliery Engineering	Geology II.

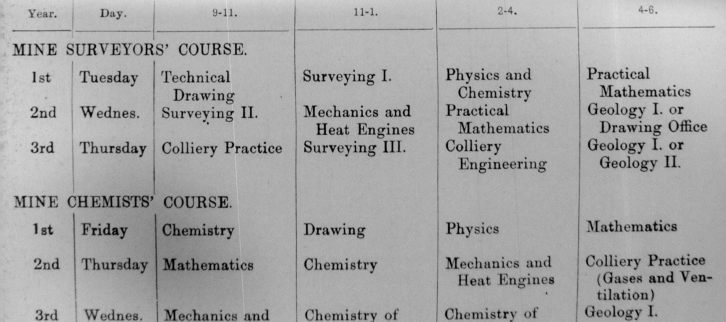

MINE SURVEYORS' COURSE.

Year.	Day.	9-11.	11-1.	2-4.	4-6.
1st	Tuesday	Technical Drawing	Surveying I.	Physics and Chemistry	Practical Mathematics
2nd	Wednes.	Surveying II.	Mechanics and Heat Engines	Practical Mathematics	Geology I. or Drawing Office
3rd	Thursday	Colliery Practice	Surveying III.	Colliery Engineering	Geology I. or Geology II.

MINE CHEMISTS' COURSE.

Year.	Day.	9-11.	11-1.	2-4.	4-6.
1st	Friday	Chemistry	Drawing	Physics	Mathematics
2nd	Thursday	Mathematics	Chemistry	Mechanics and Heat Engines	Colliery Practice (Gases and Ventilation)
3rd	Wednes.	Mechanics and Heat Engines	Chemistry of Fuels	Chemistry of Fuels	Geology I.
4th	Friday	Chemistry of Fuels	Chemistry of Fuels	Colliery Engineering (Surface Plant-preparing Coal for market)	Geology II.

29 full-time and 110 part-time students enrolled that first academic year. The first day of term was Wednesday, 8th October 1913 and the first ever class to be held, at 9.00 a.m. that day, was Chemistry for the full-time students. The class was held in the chemical laboratory on the first floor of the current Ty Crawshay at Treforest, in what is now the University's Postgraduate Centre. It was led by Mr Edgar C. Evans B.Sc. (Cardiff), Assoc. M.I.C. Mr Evans, a Ferndale (Rhondda) man, had been the Chief Chemist of the Lewis Merthyr Colliery Company before joining the School of Mines; the students probably couldn't have been in better hands.

Left: Provisional timetables showing colliery managers, mine surveyors and mine chemists' courses taken from the the first prospectus 1913

The rest of the small teaching team were:

Professor George Knox, F.G.S., M.I.M.E. – the Principal and Director of Mining; formerly Head of the Mining Department of Wigan Mining and Technical College.

John Samuel – Senior Lecturer in Mining and Assistant Director; formerly senior lecturer in Mining for Glamorgan County Council.

Fred H. Downie, BSc (Glasgow), A.R.T.C., A.M.I.E.E. – Senior Lecturer in Electrical Engineering; formerly a lecturer in electrical engineering at Glasgow Technical College.

Robert (Bobby) James, Whit.Sch., A.R.C.Sc. – Senior Lecturer in Mechanical Engineering.

Richard Richards, M.I.Inst.M.E. – Assistant Lecturer in Mining and Geology; formerly Lecturer in mining, geology and surveying and special lecturer for the Colliery Managers' Home Office Course for Glamorgan County Council.

There were certainly other staff employed in support roles but few of their identities are visible at this distance, but it is clear that the Principal had a Clerk, and that a Caretaker and his wife (who lived in a cottage on the site) looked after the buildings and even provided meals for students, and a 'laboratory boy' took care of all things miscellaneous and, no doubt, grubby.

Students

The students were drawn from across the South Wales coalfield, and were generally in the employment of the colliery companies which had founded the School and, as such, they enjoyed a discounted tuition fee. If they were in the employment of a 'non-subscribing' colliery company then they paid a tuition fee which was 25% higher. In 1913 the tuition fees were set at £10 for a full-time course, and £2. 10s for the part-time day courses. Special courses, such as those arranged for electricians, surveyors and chemists, cost £5.

The full-time fee of £10 represented a substantial commitment for a student or their family so the scholarships available would have been much sought after. The Governing Body provided two open scholarships of around £60 per year and these were based on a student's performance in their entrance examination. When awarded, they generally followed the student through to the end of his course. Part-time students, too, could win a scholarship of around £10 per year: these were offered by the neighbouring local education authorities but, unlike the full-time scholarships, were means-tested. Part-time students would have found a scholarship extremely welcome given that the men were rarely paid on the days they came to the School. There was a little extra financial help available: arrangements had been made with the Taff Vale Railway Company to provide students with half-price season tickets if they produced a voucher issued by Professor Knox.

CHRISTIAN NAME *Ke Hsün* SURNAME CHÁNG

BORN *20th October 1887.* ADMITTED *Oct. 1913.* ENTRANCE QUALIFN. *Took 1st yr Joint Diploma Course at Cardiff University*

LAST EVG. SCH. EDUCATIONAL TRAINING *3 yrs Preparatory Course } Shanghai University 4th Mining Course } China. Passed Exams under Bd of Education of China.*

ADDRESS	BOROUGH OR U D	OCCUPATION	EMPLOYER
161 Richmond Rd, Roath Park, Cardiff			

Year	Receipt No.	Student pays	Employer pays	Subject	Cl.	Subject	Cl.	Subject	Cl.	Subject	Cl.	Subject	Cl.	Subject	Cl.	Course and Year
13–14	76	£13–11–0		Mineralogy Electrotechnics	I I	Mechan'l Engine'g Geology	II I	Eng. Drawing	II	Colliery Practice " Engineering	II I	Surveying	II	Pure Maths ✱ Chem. of Fuels ✱	II I	J.D.C. 2nd yr.

NOTES ✱ *Taken at University College, Cardiff.*   PRIZES AND DISTINCTIONS.

The University of Glamorgan is fortunate in that the students' records from the Treforest School of Mines are very nearly intact. Of the reported 139 students who enrolled in that first year, 107 records have survived, including those of two students from China, Cheng Jan Wen and Ke Huan Chang. Both had previously studied at Shanghai University and enrolled on the full-time Diploma in Mining at Treforest. It may well be the case that their time at the School of Mines was designed to provide an international dimension to their studies in Shanghai since they attended the School for just one academic year and neither appeared to sit the end of year examinations. But, with limited opportunities to mix with other nationalities and cultures, the locally-based students must have found Chang and Wen infinitely exotic and interesting!

The student records are a fascinating picture of the enormous range of occupations in the coal industry at the time, and it's also interesting to see that among this student body there was a good range of seniority and experience. For example, William Griffiths was already the Under-manager of Ynysfeio Colliery in Treherbert at the start of his studies. Among the occupations of the first group of students were a timekeeper, a number of firemen and colliers, an underground measurer, a draughtsman, a ropesmith, a shotsman, a mine chemist, a ripper, a haulier and a boiler-maker.

Above, left: Still well persevered, the student record cards contain incredible minute detail regarding students, courses and their marks. Those included are just a small selection, with the University archives housing thousands more documents

THE SOUTH WALES & MON. SCHOOL OF MINES, TREFOREST,
— R.F.C., 1921-22. —

	C. G. Jones.	F. John.	W. T. Lintern.	R. Richards.	S. R. Illingworth.		
W. H. Griffiths.	F. R. Wright.	F. Winstanley.	W. H. Holt.	V. Bartholomew.	T. Davies.	F. Lloyd-Rees.	J. Hughes.	D. Beck.
E. D. Rees.	T. H. Evans.	H. Griffiths, (Vice-Capt.)	J. D. Morgan, (Capt.)	J. W. F. Povall, (Hon. Sec.)	D. M. Davies.	J. B. Elliott.

Above: the 1921-22 Rugby team

Apart from the small Chinese contingent, the men of the first student intake were almost exclusively drawn from the towns of the South Wales coalfield. The Rhondda Valleys' towns were well represented: Treorchy and Treherbert, Ferndale, Pentre, Penygraig and many more. The Cynon Valley towns of Mountain Ash and Aberdare had men in the first cohort as did Merthyr Tydfil, Treharris, and Troedyrhiw. Men from the western coalfield attended from Resolven, Port Talbot, Ystradgynlais and other towns. One student, Stanley Wang, had previously studied at the Wigan Mining College where Professor Knox had been Head of Department. Stanley appears in a photograph of the School of Mines' first rugby team of 1913-14 along with William Knox, son of the Principal and also a former student at Wigan. It's possible that Stanley decided to join his friend William in South Wales when the Knox family moved to the area.

'open to all students on equal terms...'

Of this first group of students the oldest was Tom Morgan of Bryngolau in Ferndale in the Rhondda Valley. Tom, an Overman employed by David Davies and Sons Ltd., was a mature 47 years old when he started the Colliery Managers' course. His admission to the School of Mines is an admirable thing, both from the point of view of his own aspirations and from that of the ethos of the School. It is an example that the School was keen to stick to its philosophy that its provision was 'open to all students on equal terms...'

Age clearly wasn't a factor if the student demonstrated ability and promise. The youngest of the group was Ernest James Hookway of Roath, Cardiff, who started his course in November 1913 when he was just days past his 16th birthday. Ernest was employed as a Laboratory Assistant at the School and continued studying right through the war, ending his studies in 1921 (note: Ernest may have been the same 'laboratory boy' referred to in early staff lists). The average age of the first cohort of students was almost 26 years.

Overall, the School's pride and interest in this group of students comes through clearly in these records, as someone has taken the time to later add updates to their record cards. More often than not these are about later career promotions, professional qualifications gained or learned papers published. For instance, Howell Jeffreys left his studies in 1916 and the record keeper then notes that he became a 'Pioneer Chemist in 187507 Depot', with the wartime British Expeditionary Forces in France, and that in peaceful 1920 he became a 'County Lecturer' for Glamorgan County Council. These extra details have an affectionate and proud feel about them since, in day-to-day terms, it was unnecessary to add this detail – it can only have been done because the students kept in touch with their School, and the School recorded their later successes with a parent-like pleasure.

The curriculum of 100 years ago was simple:

almost all students studied some aspect of mining

Mathematics • Chemistry • Engineering
Drawing • Surveying, Mechanics
Physics • Geology • Colliery Practice Mineralogy
Electrotechnics and Chemistry of Fuels
Colliery Engineering and practical time in the Mining Laboratory

The three-year full-time course had a broad coverage of Mathematics, Chemistry, Engineering Drawing, Surveying, Mechanics, Physics, Geology, and Colliery Practice. The second year introduced Mineralogy, Electrotechnics, and Chemistry of Fuels. The third year built on the earlier curriculum and added Colliery Engineering and practical time in the Mining Laboratory. Assessment was by way of a mixture of marks from 'Homework' and an 'Official Examination' in each subject. There was also an opportunity to gain other useful qualifications: a number of the first cohort of students studied for a St John's Ambulance qualification in first aid and one or two of them took this useful skill out to the Western Front with them in wartime service.

A part-time (day) curriculum was designed for Mine Managers, Mechanics, Electricians and Chemists which was a demanding four years in length with an eight-hour day. For Mine Surveying students the curriculum was a little kinder at three-years in length with the same eight-hour day.

'Special' courses could be organised and these appeared to be flexible arrangements to meet the needs of an individual with a curriculum designed for the purpose. For example, in the first cohort was David Thomas of Porth, Rhondda, a chemistry teacher at Porth Higher Elementary School who enrolled on a two-year special course to 'prepare for the Institute of Chemistry Examinations'.

Troubles to come:
1914-1918

These wonderful historic records are all very well but it doesn't take a lot of imagination to see that the early years of the School of Mines were 'shaky'. There was no difficulty at 'domestic' level: there was a more than adequate budget to run the place, there was every commitment and motivation for success, and an early reputation for quality was established through a government inspection in 1916. The major challenge would come from the international political crisis, with a lesser but non-stop challenge around the debate on the advanced education for miners and whether it should be at the School of Mines or the University College. But the students and their curriculum barely had time to settle when international events took the worst of turns. On 4th August 1914, at the end of the first year of the School of Mines, Britain declared war on Germany. Arguably, war was more of an accelerant to those changes in society which were already taking shape, but the micro effects of the war on the School and its student community would be acute.

Following the declaration of war, regular British soldiers and reservists were quickly despatched to areas of conflict. Lord Kitchener, Secretary of State for War, issued his famous recruiting cry "Your Country Needs You" and many – very many – men answered that call. Many words have been written about why Kitchener's call was answered by 500,000 men by mid September, but the reasons are probably fairly straightforward. There were many tales of German atrocities (nearly always fictitious) which appealed to the national sense of 'fair play'. There was also a commonly held belief that it would 'all be over by Christmas', so the opportunity for excitement and travel needed to be seized.

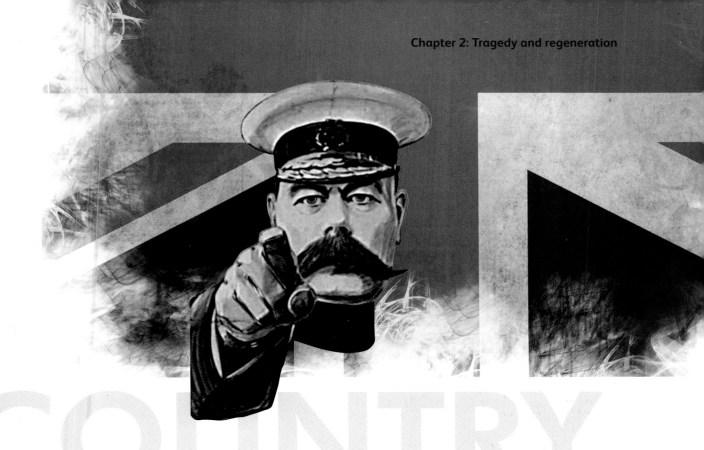

But in poorer, industrial areas there was the added incentive of a change from the daily working drudge and the struggle for a reliable wage. Meals would be provided (saving a mouth to feed at home), clothing would be supplied, and there was the chance of sending part of one's pay home. For these reasons, heavy industry and mining provided a disproportionate number of recruits to the war effort. At the School of Mines, of the students who enrolled in October 1913, 42 of them did not return for a second academic year. It's clear that some of these students must have found either combining part-time study and work too challenging or too harsh on the weekly pay packet, as a few stopped

attending before year-end. This would be perfectly normal, but the School also experienced a good proportion of students enlisting despite mining being a largely protected occupation during the war. Therefore the loss of students to military service on top of the 'normal' level of drop-out must have been a severe blow to the School. The war also strained attendances by making enormous demands on coal production and this would have affected the mine managers' ability to release men for study. So the second year's recruitment would have been a serious headache to the School's Management Board.

Student soldiers

In 1914 the School of Mines was an advanced engineering institution. Engineers were of enormous strategic and practical value to the war effort. The School also represented a pool of well educated young men, and such men were significant since they contributed enormously to the junior officer group which typically led a platoon of men. In this centenary publication, the University would most especially wish to pay tribute to the students of the School who put their ambitions and career plans on hold while they followed their belief that the honourable action at that time was to serve their country.

Looking at those students who began their course in the 1913/14 academic year but who didn't return the following year, 14 are known to have enlisted. More students went to war at a later date, and the story of the whole group may be narrated in full on another occasion, but of that 14, eight were to die in the conflict.

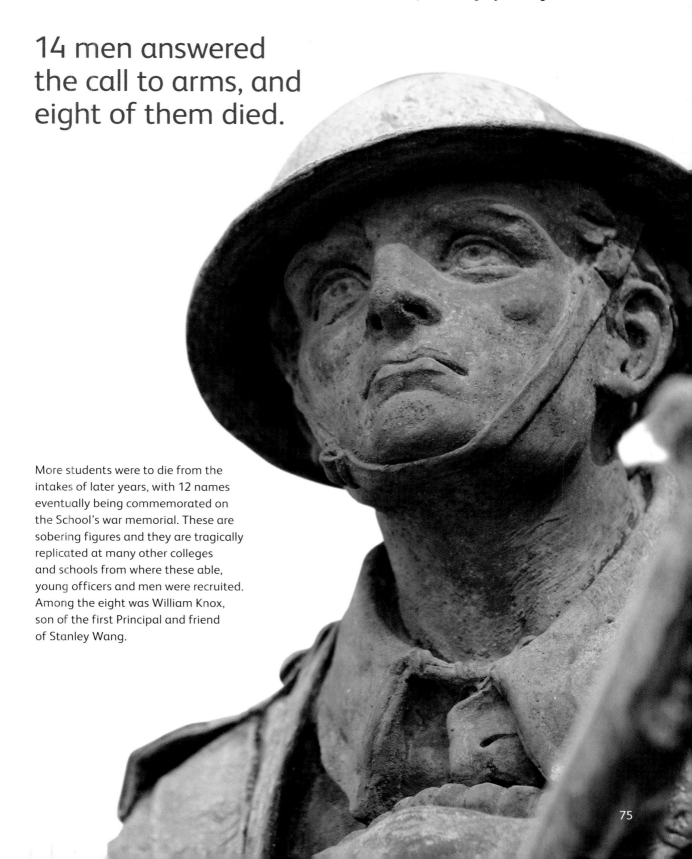

14 men answered the call to arms, and eight of them died.

More students were to die from the intakes of later years, with 12 names eventually being commemorated on the School's war memorial. These are sobering figures and they are tragically replicated at many other colleges and schools from where these able, young officers and men were recruited. Among the eight was William Knox, son of the first Principal and friend of Stanley Wang.

2nd Lieutenant William Knox

1893-1918

'...average 'flying life expectancy' of a pilot on the Western Front has been calculated as low as 93 flying hours in periods of peak combat.'

GLENBUCK. W.S.

William Knox was born in 1893 in Glenbuck, a tiny Scottish mining village now abandoned. He was the second of three children born to George and Agnes Knox: his elder brother being John, and his younger sister named Agnes, after her mother. William's family moved home at least three times; each time necessitated by his father's growing professional reputation and career advancement. Following the move to Treforest, William enrolled in the School himself as a student, perhaps with plans to build a career in the mining industry or maybe to become an academic as his father had done. The family lived in Heol Isaf in Radyr and William was active both in his studies and in sport – he was the President of the first ever rugby team of the School of Mines and he is pictured with his team in a photograph

taken before the urgencies of war swept aside many such activities.

William volunteered to train as a pilot in the Royal Flying Corps – not something to be undertaken lightly since the average life expectancy of a pilot on the Western Front has been calculated as low as 93 flying hours in periods of peak combat. As well as the obvious dangers of combat, pilot and air crew were additionally at risk from their own under-developed training programmes and the rudimentary nature of the early aircraft – with more air crew being killed at times in training accidents than in combat.

Above: The small Scottish village of Glenbuck, Ayrshire, was the birthplace of Williams Knox. The small mining village is now mostly abandoned as a result of open cast mining operations

'His sacrifice is also recorded on the Radyr village memorial and at the University where he is still thought of and where his photograph still hangs on the wall.'

EDGAR JONES
WALTER L. JENKINS
WILLIAM KNOX
VICTOR W. V. LOWRIE
TREVOR E. LEWIS
FRANCIS M. MABBITT
DOUGLAS T. MABBITT
ROBERT J. PONSFORD
DOUGLAIS P. ROBATHAN
OLIVER WATKINS

TO THE
LASTING HONOUR
OF RADYR'S
GALLANT DEAD

William was posted to 54th Squadron in Northern France early in 1918 – an extreme example of unfortunate timing as the massive German Spring Offensive was about to begin. The Spring Offensive was Germany's final concerted effort to bring the war to a victorious end while they were able to make use of the troops who had returned from the Russian front and take advantage of the short time before American troops arrived in numbers and became fully effective. It was into this arena that the inexperienced 25 year old pilot arrived to 'do his bit'. The Germans' big push meant that William's squadron returned to their low level attack missions of earlier in the war, once again exposing themselves to the risk posed from both ground fire and enemy fighter aircraft.

Until recent years it was believed that, on 26th March 1918, William, flying a Sopwith Camel C1553, took off with his squadron to take part in a patrol over the German lines. It was reported that William lagged slightly behind his colleagues and his vulnerability was spotted by Baron Manfred von Richthofen, the famous German fighter ace. Ernst Udet, another German pilot flying that day, later wrote that the British airman did not see the descending German Fokker until too late and author Floyd Gibbons, writing in 1927, says that William Knox was shot down in flames, becoming von Richthofen's 69th victim. His plane was last seen two miles south west of Peronne.

Yet recent research has confirmed that William was actually shot down and killed two days earlier, on 24th March. From the detailed notes of the German flyers' engagements, this clearly means he was not a victim of the famous Red Baron; he was killed by another or by ground fire. But it matters little. William was talented, full of promise and well-loved, but he has no known grave. Instead his name is recorded on the Arras Flying Services Memorial to the missing. His sacrifice is also recorded on the Radyr village memorial and at the University where he is still thought of and where his photograph still hangs on the wall. Possibly significantly, William's student record card no longer exists in the archive. One can only wonder whether it was removed by a sensitive and sympathetic member of staff to save his father's feelings.

William represents the group of students who were well educated and enjoyed the many opportunities that middle class life provided in the early years of the twentieth century. Other students at the School of Mines were ordinary working class colliers with a very different life style and different expectations.

Left: The Radyr war memorial commemorating the men killed in two world wars, including William Knox

Private Thomas Richard Davies Ray

1885-1915

If it's possible for a man to be more singular, among an exceptional group of men, then that is how Thomas Ray should be described. Thomas was born in Treherbert in the Rhondda on 1st of October 1885 and by the time he was 15 he was already working as a 'hewer of coal'. His was hard and dangerous work, hacking at the coal face itself. He lived in a two-up-two-down terraced house with six other lodgers *and* a family of five – a total of 12 people in all! Contemporary coalfield records suggest he would have earned about 1 shilling and 9 pence a day, or 10/6 a week. Thomas must have read one of the advertisements in the local press about the new School of Mines and decided to sit the entrance examination.

Despite the poorest of family circumstances and a shortened education, which he'd left about 14 years earlier, he reached the required standard. He enrolled on a Level One course which involved studying 'Mechanics and Heat', 'Physics and Chemistry', Colliery Practice' and 'Principles of Mathematics'. His attendance wasn't good and his marks at the end of the academic year reflect this. But Thomas, in common with many of the part-time students, would have been very lucky to be paid for the days he attended School and so perhaps he had difficult decisions to make. He worked at the Bute Colliery in Treherbert, owned by the Ocean Coal

Company and he seems to have had no financial support from his employer since Thomas paid his own tuition fees of £2 10 shillings (about 4 weeks pay). Imagine, then, how this opportunity to get an advanced education might have changed Thomas's life if war hadn't intervened.

But intervene it did, and he volunteered for service almost straight away. He enlisted in Pentre (Rhondda) and joined the Army Service Corps. The Army Service Corps (which was awarded the prefix 'Royal' in 1918) was important for continually re-supplying the materials of war, whether it was bullets or bread, and the range of their tasks was immense. Thomas was assigned to the enormous Bulford Camp on Salisbury Plain in Wiltshire which still exists today. It isn't known exactly what role he undertook at Bulford but from his Army service number it's clear he was in the Motor Transport Branch.

Above: Bute Colliery, Treherbert

Right: The gravestone of Thomas Ray

Thomas never left the UK: after little more than a year in the Army Thomas died in a tragic accident. On Sunday, 12th December 1915 he fell down stairs fracturing the base of his skull, and he died in the military hospital at the camp.

For his family and friends there may have been a crumb of consolation in that Thomas could return home and so enable them to pay respects at his graveside. He was returned to Treherbert on Thursday, 16th December and his funeral took place the following day with full military honours. Among the stories about local weddings and the Christmas show, the Rhondda Leader reported Thomas's funeral on the front page. He was attended by the Volunteer Training Corps, the Ambulance Brigade, a large company of local soldiers and the Ty Draw Brass Band. Thomas was described as being "...held in high esteem in the Upper Rhondda where he was well known".

As Thomas's gravestone in Treorchy Cemetery so quietly puts it,

'For King and for country he died. In God and in peace he lived'.

On equal terms

The University is blessed with a beautiful war memorial recording the names of all 12 students who lost their lives whilst on military service during the First World War. Every year a short and touching service is held at the memorial in Tŷ Crawshay, the original School of Mines building, to remember the men as students and to pray for peace. Besides William Knox and Thomas Ray, the other students on the memorial are:

Captain Ernest Alfred Morgan
of Aberfan, and Mountain Ash.

Captain Frank Emlyn Williams
of Merthyr Tydfil and Mountain Ash.

Lieutenant John Haydn Davies
of Blaenclydach, Rhondda.

Private David Evans
of Gelli, Ystrad, Rhondda.

Lieutenant Evan Lindsay Prichard Evans
of Mountain Ash.

Cadet Cyril J.E. Jones
of Abertillery.

Captain Thomas Glyn Llewellyn Phillips, MC
of Cardiff.

2nd Lieutenant Ernest James Phillips
of Aberdare.

May

2nd Lieutenant Eric Montagu Rees
of Cardiff.

Private Leolyn Phillips Williams
of Ton Pentre, Rhondda.

they rest in peace

Winning
the peace

In the post war years, the arguments about the fit and proper location for advanced education for miners were continually re-visited. In fact, some discussions went on right up until the first years of the Second World War. The archive documents covering the extent and repetition of these talks make exasperating and depressing reading even today, but the extent of the discussions reflects the frustrations that many in authority, the County Councils most notably, felt towards this maverick, privately funded institution. Further irritation may have followed when the School went on to volunteer itself for formal inspection by His Majesty's Inspectors of Education – and came out of the process with glowing praise for its standards.

The Treforest School of Mines was the first of the two schools to volunteer itself for inspection although, sadly, no copy of this 1915 report has been traced. However, the Crumlin School of Mines with its common Principal (George Knox) and Vice Principal (John Samuel), a common set of objectives and a 'common purse' was inspected in the spring of 1916. The team of three inspectors from the Board of Education unequivocally endorsed the 'sandwich' system of education which had been impossible for the University College to implement. The report says *"...that the School is in intimate association with the collieries is one of its most valuable and important features from the standpoint of the student, since it enables him to study the scientific aspect of the various problems of the mine under practical conditions."* Although these reports were, at the time, confidential, the view of the inspection team would have been known and must have resulted in further debate at the University College: sandwich vocational education was important, highly recommended and unavoidable, but it would still be some years before it was introduced at the University College in Cardiff.

Overall the tenor of the report is extremely positive with almost every important aspect receiving praise. The inspectors finish with very strong recommendations about development of a coordinated scheme of mining education to cover the whole coalfield but this is a political, not a quality-related, point. The School of Mines had been measured and not found wanting.

Back at Treforest, the trials of the war years were weathered and the returning servicemen were hungry for education. It may be that their war experiences had shown them that life's opportunities

were there to be grasped or lost, and the numbers of men enrolling in the post war years seem to bear this out. Given that the Armistice was signed in November 1918 and many men had to wait in turn to be demobilised, academic year 1919-20 is when the 'peace dividend' reached the School. In 1919, 338 students enrolled compared to 191 the year before; an enormous increase of 177%. These abnormal conditions lasted three years and then numbers slowly reduced year on year toward 1926, the year of the general strike.

Startlingly, the Board of Management of the two Schools put them forward for their second inspection slap bang in the middle of the General Strike. It's hard to imagine why when the situation couldn't have been more difficult, unless it was a hint that a 'plan B' might be needed for the future of the Schools. That is, the Board might have anticipated a good inspection report prior to an attempt to hive off the Schools to new owners and shed the now burdensome cost. But if that was the motivation then it was a risky strategy since the full-time students couldn't have completed the normal practical elements of their study and part-time students (working miners) had not a penny to spend on fares to Treforest. But possibly the most risky

aspect of an inspection at this time was that the School had no steady income. The School had been funded by a levy applied to every ton of coal produced in the coalfield, and no coal meant no money unless it was as a direct gift from the pockets of the Coal Owners themselves. There certainly wasn't any routine revenue – would this impact on the inspection?

The evaporation of the budget hadn't happened at the time of the inspection, although it is clearly anticipated and the inspectors write about the problem in their report. The report praises the research, the equipment (often specially designed and made for the School in its own workshops), the teaching staff and their qualifications, and the student societies. There are minor anxieties about the new wing (new in 1913) which needs a coat of paint, some laboratories are said to be cold and a better common room for students is needed. But the major concern, once again, is around the lack of a multi-level, coordinated scheme of mining.

Overall the report, at this key point in the School's history, states that the Governors are to be congratulated for having "…inaugurated and subsequently maintained one of the best, if not the best, equipped Schools of Mines in the country [which] has now established itself." The Schools of Mines, both of them, were going to need a good reference behind them as they were about to be in the market for new owners.

Put simply, the General Strike of 1926 came about following a series of testy negotiations and industrial actions which had tried to protect miners against cuts in wages the employers felt were essential as coal prices fell after the War. For the School of Mines the obvious consequence of the lengthy strike was that between May and December 1926 almost no coal had been produced which, in turn, meant that its funding dried up. The Coal Owners were no longer in a position to fund the School, so a new solution to paying for it had to be found, and fast.

The options available were to close the School, to give it to the University College where it may have become a department, or to transfer ownership from private hands to public ownership through Glamorgan County Council. On Tuesday, 10 April 1928, less than 15 years after the opening of the School, a meeting took place with key representatives of the local authorities; the University College; the University of Wales; the Central Committee of the Miners' Welfare Fund; and the School of Mines' Board of Management. An almost verbatim account of this meeting survives, showing it to be tense in the extreme.

Below, right: Volumes of minutes and meeting books from education committees and councils, still intact and housed in the University archives

Mr Hugh Ingledew, a Cardiff solicitor and Secretary to the Board of Management of the School, laid it on the line, saying

"The governing bodies have now decided to close the schools on 31st August [1928] and the staff have been given notice. The constituent members have been finding £11,000 per year. It must be taken as definite that the coal owners are not prepared to carry on the school indefinitely, with the pious hope that the LEAs or the University will take it."

In addition,

"… the coal owners are going nowhere after 31st August, and many students are in the middle of their course at present, and they [the County Councils] must make arrangements for these students almost immediately."

It is clear from the language used and the terseness of the report that this was it, the brink, and a decision about the continuance of the School was going to be made on this day.

The centenary year of education at Treforest is the clearest indication that the outcome of the meeting was the right one. The local authorities, Monmouthshire County Council and Glamorganshire County Council, took over the management and funding of the Crumlin School and the Treforest School respectively. Crumlin went on to become a part of Crosskeys College but its building, badly affected by subsidence, was demolished in 1967. Treforest, as we will see, remained a successful School of Mines and went on to grow in size and reputation in the decades to come.

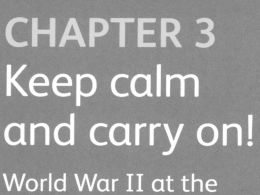

CHAPTER 3
Keep calm and carry on!

World War II at the South Wales and Monmouthshire School of Mines

The devastating results of the three nights blitz on Swansea's High Street and College Street

With the School's funding from the Coal Owners' companies coming to an abrupt halt and the School transferring into the ownership of Glamorganshire County Council, the inter-war years had proved none too peaceful for the School of Mines. Although his portrait represents him looking serene and untroubled Professor Knox, who guided the School through this difficult time, must have been sorely tried during much of his tenure. Following his retirement in 1931, Robert (Bobby) James took over, firstly as 'Acting Principal' and later confirmed in his post. It was Mr James' turn to manage the School's development and the politics of education in the South Wales area – challenging enough in its own right without adding another world war into the mix.

One might have expected the School's relationship with the University College to have reached a state of equilibrium after its change of management, but this was not so. Some grumblings, and some more constructive discussions, about the place of the School went up to and past the moment when Prime Minister Chamberlain returned from Munich waving his piece of paper and declaring 'peace in our time'. But nothing came of this and the School entered the war years still under the management of Glamorganshire County Council.

So, what did the School look and feel like at this landmark moment in history?

Campus

The campus was much the same as in its founding year; based in the building which is now known as Tŷ Crawshay. Immediately adjacent to the house were numerous barns and outbuildings and these became used as storage or workshop space and, later, as a base for the Home Guard battalion (Dad's Army) which was based on the campus. During the war some limited building would take place to accommodate the influx of soldier-students, and everyone had use of a playing field for sports – this latter facility being a left-over from the days when the campus had

TABLE TENNIS TEAM, 1941–42.

Front Row: K. Lee.   G. Everleigh (*Vice-Capt.*).   L. Wookey (*Capt. & Sec.*).   T. H. Thomas (*President*).   W. Wicks.
Second Row: J. C. Williams.   T. Short.   J. Thomas.   T. C. Coombes.
Back Row: J. Jones.   A. Hanford.   A. V. Williams.

SCHOOL OF MINES R.F.C., 1939-40.

Back Row (*Left to Right*) : M. M. Jenkins.   C. Evans.   J. Pullen.   G. Eveleigh.
Second Row : L. R. Thomas (*Gen. Sec.*).   C. K. Trotman.   G. Smith.   G. T. Bolan (*Trainer*).   D. Pugh.   W. J. Thomas.   A. R. Fox (*Gen. Treas.*).
Front Row : W. A. Howard.   D. M. Dummer.   W. G. Thomas (*Capt.*).   Mr. Robert James (*Principal*).   R. R. Williams (*Vice-Capt.*).
B. Hunt (*Secr.*).   L. Walker.

been a farm and the house was named Forest House. The playing field lay to the north of the School's building and served another useful wartime purpose with its grass crop being used as animal fodder by a local farmer, who paid two guineas annually for the privilege. It was eventually forfeited when the Brecon Building (B Block) was built in the early 1960s. Further north, approximately where the Students Services department is in 2013, was a fine circle of standing stones. Erection of the circle has been attributed to Francis Crawshay, and this seems extremely likely as it included a large central pillar on which was inscribed in a random order the names of various members of his family, the earliest of which dated back to 1650. In some places the circle is described as a Gorsedd stone circle, constructed when the National Eisteddfod takes place in the locality. However, this isn't the case as the 1893 Gorsedd circle was located on the Common in Pontypridd. Sadly, despite lengthy consideration of alternative options, the Treforest stones were broken up around 1962 to clear the space for further building.

The School has always had a thriving sporting community, shown above with the 1939-1940 School of Mines rugby team, and left, the 1941-42 table tennis team

The garden in front of Tŷ Crawshay had existed from the days of Francis Crawshay's ownership, but in 1920 it had acquired the wonderful beam engine from the defunct Newbridge Colliery at Gelliwion, Pontypridd. The garden and engine were frequently used as a backdrop for group photographs during the war in a similar way to their use as a backdrop for students' graduation photographs today. They were, and remain to this day, a well-loved feature of the University.

Above, left: Built in 1845 by Varteg Ironworks, the Beam Engine in its original location at the Newbridge Colliery, Pontypridd and pictured both from the time and at its present home on the Treforest campus grounds

Flashback, 1939

"It's no good bringing these things here, we still use
the old oil lamp"

Management

1939-40

The School of Mines was under the management of Glamorganshire County Council's *'Management Sub-Committee of the School of Mines, Treforest'*. The group comprised of five Aldermen, four County Councillors, one Rhondda Councillor and one representative of the Coal Owners (the coal industry wasn't nationalised at that time). It seems extraordinary from a modern perspective that the Principal, Mr James, was not a member of this Management Sub-Committee, but he was able to provide input to their meetings by furnishing the Director of Education with a report which was then quoted from for the benefit of the committee members.

Mr James' reports covered a broad range of matters. At the important end of the scale he recommended on the continuance of students' scholarships and their academic progress. At the more mundane end of the scale, Mr James reported on purchases which had been made as a matter of urgency – in December 1939 it was 40 gallons of fuel oil and reference books to the value of £1. 5. 9. Supplies which were less urgent needed the approval of the Management Sub-Committee and examples of these include laboratory chemicals, spring balances and boxwood rules for the Engineering Department, and office stationery.

The pay scales of Mr James' staff were set by the Committee, which also considered applications for pay rises. For example, in July 1940 the pay of three workshop staff was reviewed, and Principal James made a strong case for an increase by comparing the men's pay (£3. 16. 0. per week) to that of the *'instructors and demonstrators at the Government Training Centre at Treforest which pays £5. 17. 6. for a 37 hour working week and where there are vacancies for nine on the staff'*. He was clearly seeing a real chance of losing good staff to this nearby organisation. But he didn't win his case: the Committee were only prepared to offer a pretty measly rounding up of their pay to £4 per week – a rise of just four shillings.

Left: A 'flashback' cartoon from the 1945/1946 Breccia student magazine

In the 26 years since the School first enrolled students there were no seismic changes in the courses offered. There had been a gradual broadening of the range of subjects (to include Motor Engineering, Building and Accountancy, for example) but any member of staff from 1913 who managed to time-shift to 1939 would have recognised most of the courses – at least by subject title. The content, of course, had moved forward with changing technologies and updated approaches to safety in coal mines. The courses for the 1939-40 academic year were:

For Full-time Students:

Mining Engineering (in conjunction with University College, Cardiff)

Engineering (a combined course in Mechanical and Electrical Engineering)

Chemical Engineering

Surveying and Prospecting Diploma

Preparatory Science

For Part-time Day Students:

Colliery Managers

Surveying

Mechanical Engineering

Surveying (Post Certificate)

Electrical Engineering

Technical Chemists

Mining Electrical Engineering

Gas Engineering

For Evening Students:

Safety in Mines Class

Mining Electrical Engineering

Senior Courses (SI, SII & SIII)

Handicraft (Woodwork & Metalwork)

Mine Chargemen and Firemen

Motor Engineering

Surveying

Workshop Practice

Mining, Advanced

Gas Supply

Mechanical Engineering

National Certificate in Commerce

Electrical Engineering

Secretarial & Accountancy Course

Foundry Practice

Preliminary Technical Classes

Building and Quantities (Part I & II)

1939-40

Curriculum

In the passing of a generation there were a couple of experienced 'constants' in the staff. Mr James, the Principal, was on the original teaching team as Senior lecturer in Mechanical Engineering in 1913 as was Richard Richards who was then an Assistant Lecturer in Mining and Geology. At the outbreak of war the number of lecturers had increased to match the higher numbers of students and the broader range of courses. They were:

Department of Mining and Mine Surveying:

Richard Richards, MSc., M.I.Min.E. (now Head of Department)

W.J.Jones, F.G.S., M.I.Min.E.

Thomas Powell, MSc., M.I.Min.E.

Department of Engineering:

H. A. Warren, MSc. (Eng.), A.M.I.C.E., A.M.I. Struct. E. (Head of Department)

R.M. Metcalfe, A.R.C.S.

H. A. Boultbee, A.M.I.Mech.E.

W. H. Blythe, A.M.I.E.E.

John B. J. Higham, M.I.E.E., A.M.I.Mech.E.

F. W. Johnson, MSc., Ph.D., A.M.I.E.E.

W.A.T. McCarthy, A.M.I.Mech.E.

Department of Fuel Technology and Chemical Engineering:

Sidney B. Watkins, MSc., F.I.C., A.M.I.Chem. E. (Head of Department)

Henry Gethin Davey, MSc., A.I.C.

Department of Mathematics:

Mr Robert James (the Principal, and Head of Department)

Cyril C. Evans, MSc.

H. M. Watkins, BSc. Econ.

The permanent team was supplemented by 'visiting lecturers' who were engaged for a specific number of hours each year to teach:

Commerce: R. V. Hoggins, J. T. Roberts, E.G. Mort, Trefor Thomas, and G.H. Jones

Building: T. Hill

Handicraft: J. Lloyd Evans, W. Tomkins, and Howard Griffiths,

English: B. Howell and J. Jones

French: P. R. Jones

Foundry Practice: J. F. Gist and E. G. Kelly.

Staff

Students

The start of academic year 1939-40 was obviously a little different to previous years. Just as would-be students were considering sitting the School's entrance examinations, on 1st September Hitler's armies invaded Poland, having invaded Czechoslovakia earlier in the spring. Britain declared war on Germany two days later on 3rd September. It's the kind of event that changes plans of men, companies, schools, colleges and governments. Given both these events and the obvious uncertainties about what was to come, it isn't at all surprising that the number of students enrolling in September 1939 was just 443. The previous year, when optimism was still available to the rosy-minded, a record number of students had enrolled: 710 in total. It's interesting to speculate

The women were:

Mildred Betty Langdon

enrolled in September 1941 on a course in Electrical Engineering. She lived at Llanbradach and worked as a 'Pyrometer Assistant' for the Northern Aluminium Company. She was the only woman who enrolled that year and the first ever female student. Betty Everson (as she is now) lives in Newport and she explains that she struggled to cope with the way engineering was taught since it was largely focussed on mining engineering – a long way from her own type of plant engineering. Betty recalls being wholly supported during her studies and particularly recalls the help she received from her Mathematics teacher. She describes her fellow students as 'quite gentlemanly'.

Rebecca Levy

enrolled on the Technical Chemistry course in September 1942. She lived at Park Place, Gilfach, Bargoed and worked as a Laboratory Apprentice for Powell Duffyn Coal Company. As Betty didn't continue her studies into a second year, Rebecca, too, was the only woman student of her day.

Sylvia Fay Howland

enrolled in September 1944 onto the Preliminary Technical Course, Part II. She was from Pontypridd and worked as a records clerk for Copygraph Ltd. on the new Treforest Trading Estate which had opened in 1936 with a very small number of companies.

whether this dramatic drop in numbers was because the men chose to remain at work, whether they anticipated being called up for military service, or whether perhaps employers were unable to release their men for part-time study as it was important to increase production to meet the demands of war.

The students who began their courses in 1939 were all men, and all were local – travelling to the School from all areas of Glamorgan, the Rhondda Valleys, and with a small number from Cardiff and Gwent.

One of the most interesting and, hopefully, welcome effects of the war, which was to be felt within a year or two of its commencement, was the arrival of the first women students. They arrived in tiny numbers, just one or two a year from 1941 onward, although Principal James had tried to establish a class for women engineers the year before but without luck. The earliest women students must have been such special people – it was, after all, a wholly male environment at the time. From the documents and plans of the building it doesn't even appear to have been blessed with a women's lavatory!

Elizabeth Jones was from Aberkenfig, near Bridgend and was 24 in 1944 when she enrolled on a part-time course in Electrical Engineering. She worked at the time as a statistics assistant for South Wales Power Company.

Whether it was as a result of the predictable strains of combining part-time study and full-time work, being (in some cases) the only woman in a male institution or, as Betty says, finding that the teaching was still centred around mining, none of the women completed their courses. However they can truly be said to be pioneers of women's engineering education.

Gwyneth Mary Mann enrolled as a part-time student in September 1944 and studied Electrical Engineering until 1947. She lived at Gelli Lwch, Graigwen in Pontypridd and worked as an Assistant Switchboard Attendant for the South Wales Power Company. Gwyneth, still living in Pontypridd, recalls that she was the only female engineer at the very large local power station – which at the time caused her mother some grave concerns; not least about what clothes to wear! Whilst studying, Gwyneth at least had the company of two other women in 1944-45, Sylvia Howland and Elizabeth Jones. In 1949 Gwyneth married a fellow student of the School of Mines, Brian Sheryn – it's believed that Gwyneth and Brian were the first student couple to marry.

Students

" What is a student, daddy ? " Somewhat startled by the unusual question, I looked up from my book to meet the enquiring eyes of my small daughter. Knowing that an answer was absolutely necessary, if I were to be permitted to continue the enjoyment of my book, I feverishly racked my brains for a simple and workable definition of a student such as might satisfy the insatiable curiosity of a four year old girl. I could easily have described a particular student but a general definition of the general student completely escaped me.

I tried to concentrate on students in the mass. I conjured up pictures of large classes to which I have lectured in the past in order that I might extract therefrom some synthesis that would characterise students as a whole. But my efforts were vain. I slowly began to realise that the student in general was something imponderable.

Always my general picture was destroyed by the intrusion of some particular student; the bright student; the dull one; the student who sits in the front row and asks all the questions, or the student who creeps to the rear hoping that his slumbers will remain undetected by the lecturer.

I recalled my first class; a part time evening class of apprentice gasfitters. There was a red haired boy who always brought an apple which he ate audibly finally discharging the inedible portion at his fellow students. The same class contained the pair who explained that owing to the times of the trains they would not be able to attend until 7.15, and maintained this fiction until the evening I caught them at 6.45 behind a couple of pints in the " Waggon and Horses." Thus was developed my interest in railway timetables.

The years passed and I was a lecturer in a Northern University and a young Indian student fresh from Madras was asking me to show him the position of the sparking plug in the steam engine . . . . . . but at this point I was brought to earth by an insistant " What is a student, daddy ? " Realising by this time that no further delay would be tolerated, I hastily and rather lamely explained that a student was a big boy, who, having finished school, entered a college in order to learn something useful. I could perceive by the contemptuous gleam in her eye that my answer was completely inacceptable, but I was saved further questioning by the timely intrusion of Jock, our neighbour's Scottie, who immediately claimed all her attenion and I turned with a sigh of relief to the enjoyment of my book.

But although my eyes resumed the scanning of the printed pages, my mind refused to occupy itself with their contents. I was disturbed by my failure to answer such a simple question. I had a feeling that I had dealt shabbily with the whole body of students, past and present. So, closing my now useless book with a snap that produced a startled wuff ! from the Scottie, I settled down to conjure up more worthy memories of the student world.

At last they came, real symbols of the use of the student youth.

There was the student conference way back in those tense days of peace between the wars. A young Austrian student from Vienna had the

32

rostrum . Himself, a fugitive from the Nazi terror in central Europe, he spoke of the stupid brutalities of the Nazi gangsters and implored the British students to join with their continental brothers in a united protest against this menace to their peace and freedom. I remember the eager sympathy in the faces of the conference delegates and the mighty applause as the resolution of protest was passed.

I recalled the long talk I had in " The Brighton Cafe " with a young prematurely aged student from Prague. It was a glorious Autumn day with the sun shimmering in a mirror-like sea. But the usual holiday crowds were absent and in their place groups of soldiers laying the first rolls of barbed wire to remind us of Dunkirk, and of the danger that was now so near. I could picture the mixture of anguish and hatred in his deep lined face as he described the horror of the year he had spent in the notorious concentration camp at Buchenwald, the daily beatings and the monstrous indignities with which the scum of Hitler's Germany sought to break the spirit of those who preferred death to slavery.

Next, came thoughts of Spain and the first fascist bombs, first beginnings of the war against innocent women and children, grim unheeded forewarnings of the future fate of Warsaw, Rotterdam, Coventry and London. British students played a man's part in this unequal combat. Uncalled, they went to give blow for blow with the murderers of peace and freedom, and many never returned. Britain lost many fine student sons in those first outpost battles of the present war.

And from Norway, too, came stories of student heroism. Scores of students facing death at the hands of the firing squads rather than co-operate with the traitors who had sold their country to the foreign invader.

Everywhere, students are in the vanguard of the fight for freedom and democracy; waging in common, a struggle against the common and brutal foe; forging close bonds of friendship between the students of the Allied Nations and guaranteeing the firm friendship of the peoples in the peace that will follow victory.

Thus, I attempted to distil the essence of the student from the questions of a child. It is for the reader to judge how far I have succeeded.

J.J.

* * * *

The oftener you look back, the quicker you won't get there.

* * * *

You can lead a boy to a college, but you cannot make him think.

* * * *

Wonderful is the intuition of woman—when it is too late.

33

A thoughtful piece on the significance of students in peace and conflict, written by a member of staff in the last years of world war two

What War?

In the early months, during the time of what became known as the 'Phoney War' between September 1939 and May 1940, the School appears to have wholly adopted the mandate to 'Keep Calm and Carry On' as there was little apparent disruption. There are understated mentions of 'the present difficulties' in the archives and even before the declaration of war the ingenious Principal, Mr James, managed to squeeze the cost of new blinds for the whole School from the County Council stressing '… the importance of replacing defective blinds…and providing new ones where there are none at present in view of possible A.R.P. requirements' – all at a cost of £96.00. Smoothly done, Mr James! But other than this wily acquisition, there is little to suggest the level of disruption to come – no sense of anxiety but instead an attitude of 'business as usual'.

The usual business for the July 1939 meeting of the Management Sub-Committee was to consider each scholarship student and, based on their progress, make the decision whether they should retain the scholarship. The level of personal and family detail placed before the management Sub-Committee appears invasive and wholly inappropriate by today's standards but it does throw a light on the background of the men who were studying at that time. For example, John E. Beanland of Maes-y-Dderwen, Nelson, was studying Part II of the Colliery Engineering course. The Committee was informed

"Father deceased. Mother receives £120 per annum from Powell Duffryn Colliery Co. for education and maintenance of applicant since death of father, plus house rent. Two children (Junior Draughtsman, Powell Duffryn Co., earning £1. 10. 0. per week), and 17 (applicant). Grandmother, who resides with Mrs Beanland, contributes 10/- per week."

war?

So, on the eve of war, rather than looking forward and fretting over the world-changing events to come, the management of the School was cosily occupied with micro level of detail about new blinds and the personal details of each student. One of the few references to any sort of disruption comes at the end of the year in the students' annual magazine 'Breccia'. The Editor, with a calm air of under-statement, says

"This year has, of course, been rather overshadowed by the war and, since a large number of students are of military age, the School has taken rather longer than usual to settle down."

This quiet feeling wouldn't last – historians regard May 1940 as marking the end of the 'Phoney War' and this is certainly the feel of the School at that time. By July 1940 the official reports and minutes reflect that war and its effects had now become a major preoccupation.

Below: Copies of the student magazine of the University, 'Breccia'

The School at War

Students appear to have enthusiastically taken on additional activities or responsibilities, keen to 'do their bit' for the country's war effort. For example, in November 1939 the Students Representative Council approached Mr James with a plan to set up an Officer Cadet Corps at the School which was to be led by Mr (later Major) Sid Watkins, Head of Fuel Technology and Chemical Engineering. But they were ahead of the game and the War Office replied that '... all commissions in future will be granted to men who have served in the ranks'.

So the plan was reluctantly dropped. However the War Office didn't take too long to change its mind and recognise its need for first class, trained young men such as those studying at the School.

Staff also responded to the emergency and were prepared to make changes and sacrifices, although these had a difficult knock-on effect on the School. For example, by July 1940 three experienced members of staff had been diverted from teaching to 'engage on war service'. Mr McCarthy from the Department of Engineering became Assistant Works Manager for

Shepherds Foundry at Bridgend. Mr Boultbee from the same department worked as a Senior Production Officer for the Ministry of Supply at Bristol, and Mr Davey swapped the Department of Fuel Technology and Chemical Engineering to become Plant Engineer at the 'Pembrey Factory', a Royal Ordnance establishment making TNT and ammonium nitrate. It is easy to see how the in-depth, specialist knowledge of the staff could be requisitioned 'for the duration'.

These absences, of course, had to be borne, as no objection could be made and the individuals themselves wouldn't have dreamed of doing so. However, the School had to work out how to get hold of alternative teachers to cover the curriculum but keep jobs open for the individuals who would return at the end of hostilities. The School was fortunate: two experienced, recently retired members of staff, Mr W. Firth and Mr R. Metcalfe still lived in the area and were able to stand in.

The School lost students to the services – and gained students from the services: all in all, something of a 'revolving door' with soldiers and would-be soldiers passing each other!

The stories of two students, Alan Holloway and Robert Thomas, are fairly typical of wartime experiences and they represent the two variations of service and later careers: one interrupted his studies to serve with the forces and later returned, whilst the other served as an essential-skilled worker in the coal mines before dramatically changing career direction at the end of the war.

The devastating results of the three nights blitz on Swansea's Castle Street

Alan Holloway's story is based on his own recollections:

Alan is from Porthcawl, and in his second year at the School (1942-43) he was lucky enough to win a Glamorgan County Scholarship worth £60 per year plus payment of his fees. He studied as a full-time student and worked for the Royal Ordnance Factory at Bridgend during the vacations. His engineering course was four years long with the option to progress to an external BSc degree of London University. As a student, Alan was also a keen sportsman, sometimes playing rugby in the morning and football in the afternoon on a busy weekend!

He has many recollections of the School, including that, in 1942, there was no facility for meals but Mr Stone the Caretaker (who doubled up as Librarian) sold tea and buns in the library at lunchtime. Deservedly or not, Mr Stone soon became the subject of a student ditty:

There is a saying that's well known,

"You can't get blood out of a stone"

But in the School of Mines we see,

that out of Stone we get weak tea!

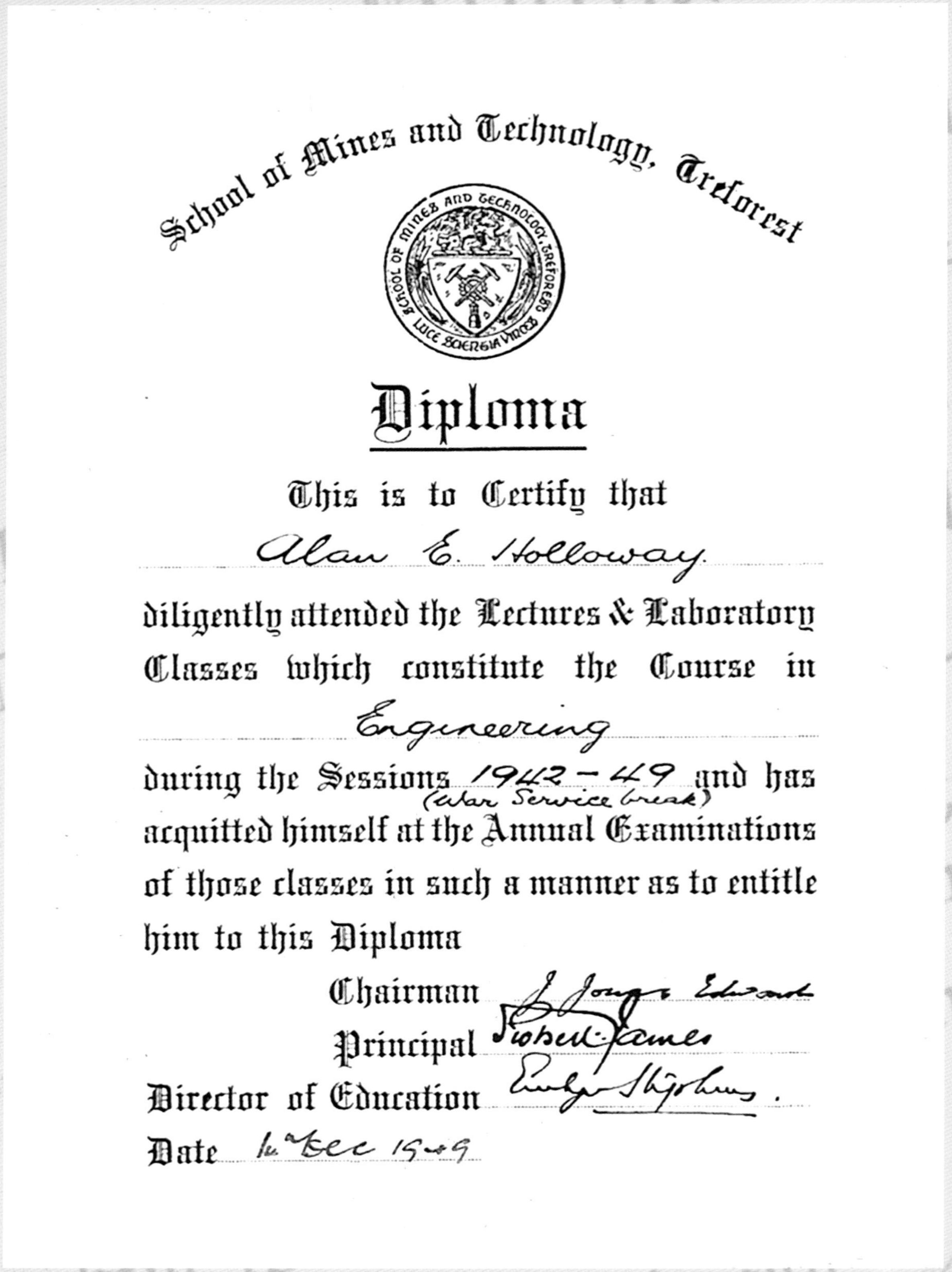

School of Mines and Technology, Treforest

Diploma

This is to Certify that

Alan E. Holloway

diligently attended the Lectures & Laboratory Classes which constitute the Course in

Engineering

during the Sessions *1942 – 49* and has *(War Service break)* acquitted himself at the Annual Examinations of those classes in such a manner as to entitle him to this Diploma

Chairman *J. Jones Edward*

Principal *Robert James*

Director of Education *Evelyn Skipobins.*

Date *16th Dec 1949*

After just one year of studies Alan interrupted his time at the School to serve in the Royal Navy for the duration of the war. His service took him around the world, to the Far East via the shore bases of HMS Royal Arthur (formerly Butlins holiday camp in Skegness!) and HMS Shrapnel (formerly the South Western Hotel in Southampton). Alan says war service can have lingering effects – by which he means the malaria which returned to trouble him from time to time, including during his final examinations which he took on his return to the School wearing an overcoat and scarf!

On his return to the School in 1946, Alan recalls the many shortages which were the legacy of war. Accommodation for students was in short supply and, on his return after 3 years naval service, Alan and eleven other students found accommodation in a local miners' hostel which was nothing more than a Nissen hut. After military service this would have been bearable. However, the winter of 1947 was famously severe – from January through to March snow drifted up to the first floor windowsills of the School. His hostel accommodation had no heat and no hot food, so Alan made his way to the School only to find he was the only student to arrive.

Above: Alan Holloway (front row, first left) pictured with the Royal Navy

Left: Alan Holloway's School of Mines and Technology diploma from 1949, which also shows the period of his studies inclusive of war service

Fortunately a canteen had been added by then so he was warmed and fed. In Alan's post-war second year he recalls there were 17 students in the Nissen hut including William Grove who had been called up for service as a Bevin Boy. Bevin Boys were young men who were conscripted but, instead of joining the armed services, they served in the mines through a scheme named after its creator Ernest Bevin, the Minister for Labour and National Service. Another friend who felt the long-lasting effects of war service was Ray Trenberth from Ystrad, Rhondda. Ray was conscripted into the Royal Navy and served a lengthy five years; experiencing difficulties at the end of his course finding an employer willing to take on a trainee who was, by now, thirty years of age.

Above: Alan (front row, second from left) at Wolverhampton Technical College

Right: Alan's hard work and determination culminated in him obtaining his National Diploma in Mechanical Engineering

NATIONAL DIPLOMA IN MECHANICAL ENGINEERING
AWARDED BY
THE INSTITUTION OF MECHANICAL ENGINEERS
IN CONJUNCTION WITH
THE MINISTRY OF EDUCATION

HIGHER GRADE

THIS is to CERTIFY that ALAN ERNEST HOLLOWAY has completed an approved FULL-TIME COURSE OF INSTRUCTION IN MECHANICAL ENGINEERING at with special reference to Marine Engineering at Glamorgan Technical College, Treforest, and has satisfied the Assessors appointed by the Institution of Mechanical Engineers in the Final Examination.

SUBJECTS OF EXAMINATION

Mathematics,
Strength of Materials,
Electrotechnics,
Engineering Design,
Mechanical Engineering, (Distinction)
Colliery Engineering,
Heat Engines.

H. Dough
President of the Institution of
Mechanical Engineers

Nicholas James
Permanent Secretary of the Welsh
Department of the Ministry of Education

Principal of Glamorgan Technical College, Treforest,

Dated this third day of August, 19 49.

Endorsed for Marine
Engineering by ....
President of the Institute of Marine Engineers.

CONDITIONS OF AWARD OF THIS DIPLOMA

National Diplomas in Mechanical Engineering of the Institution of Mechanical Engineers in conjunction with the Ministry of Education certify that the holders have passed successfully through an extended Course of Instruction in Mechanical Engineering and have passed the examination at its termination.

The Diplomas are awarded only to full-time students who have—

1. Attended courses of instruction in Establishments for Further Education jointly approved for this purpose in respect of standards of admission, equipment, qualifications of staff, curriculum and syllabus by the Institution and the Ministry.

2. Made not less than 60 per cent. of the possible attendances in each year of the course.

3. Obtained not less than 40 per cent. of the possible marks in each subject in the Final Examination.

4. Obtained not less than 40 per cent. of the possible marks for home work, class work and laboratory work in each subject in the final year of the course.

5. Obtained not less than 50 per cent. of the grand total of marks in the final year of the course.

(Distinction in a subject is awarded to successful candidates who gain not less than 85 per cent. of the possible marks in the Final Examination in that subject, and when such distinctions are awarded they are shown on the diplomas.)

THE SUBJECTS OF THE COURSE WERE :—

First Year :	Second Year :	Third Year :
Mathematics,	Pure Mathematics,	Mathematics,
Physics,	Applied Mathematics,	Structures,
Electrical Physics,	Physics,	Engineering Design,
Mechanics,	Engineering Chemistry,	Electrotechnics,
Inorganic Chemistry,	Engineering Drawing,	Heat Engines,
Geometry and	Electrotechnics,	Mechanical Engineering,
Drawing.	Mechanics and Heat	Strength of Materials,
	Engines,	Surveying.
	Structures,	
	Engineering Design.	

FOURTH YEAR

Mathematics; Strength of Materials; Electrotechnics; Engineering Design; Mechanical Engineering; Colliery Engineering; Heat Engines.

Robert Thomas

Robert Thomas's story (based on his son Dr Ceri Thomas's biography of his father)

Robert Thomas's son Ceri Thomas was also a student at the University. Between 2002 and 2007, he studied for a PhD by Portfolio. Titled 'Placing Zobole: Ernest Zobole and the Imaging of South Wales within the Visual Culture of Wales since 1945', his doctorate focused upon the Rhondda-born painter Ernest Zobole many of whose key paintings are owned by the University and with whom Robert Thomas studied at Cardiff College of Art in the late 1940s.

By early 1941 so many young men had either volunteered for the services or been conscripted that the shortage of skilled labour in some industries was acute. The Essential Work (General Provisions) Order of March 1941 required all skilled workers to register, something which allowed the Ministry of Labour to prevent them leaving jobs designated as essential to the war effort. Mining was just such a job.

Robert John Roydon Thomas enrolled at the School of Mines and Technology in September 1942 on a part-time course in Electrical Engineering – he was then working as an Assistant Electrician for the Ocean Coal Company. After one year of study, Robert had to interrupt his studies for what turned out to be a period of five years as his work was classed as essential under the 1941 Order. However, Robert had other skills and passions and, from his own words written later, he had clearly seen enough of the coal mines:

"The grim atmosphere of the work in the mines pervaded everything, and the relentless pressure of work was maintained only at the dreadful prospect of poverty should that unending labour cease."

Left: 'Miners family statue' situated in Tonypandy in the Rhondda Valley by Robert Thomas

Although he'd followed the traditional route into mining, as a child Robert had excelled in the arts. As a boy he had modelled and carved – taking clay from the river and transforming it into animal shapes which he baked in his mother's oven. So given his feelings about working in the mines, together with his passion for creating, it isn't surprising that the end of his war service prompted Robert to change direction.

In 1947, like many other ex-servicemen, Robert was entitled to a government grant to study and he chose to study sculpture at the Cardiff College of Art. In 1949 he won a scholarship to the Royal College of Art, graduating in 1952. Three years later he exhibited at the Royal Academy's Summer Exhibition for the first time. In the Fifties he began to produce his "free figure" series of statues and in 1963, he won a national competition with a monumental 'Mother and Child' for the Leicestershire town of Coalville. At around the same time he began a series of sculptures of distinguished "Welsh contemporaries". Among these portrait busts were politicians Aneurin Bevan and Viscount Tonypandy; Rhondda writer Gwyn Thomas; opera stars Sir Geraint Evans and Dame Gwyneth Jones, and rugby heroes Carwyn James and Cliff Morgan. Robert continued with this famous series for the rest of his life, making just two exceptions to his Welsh-only list – one of which was of Diana, Princess of Wales, who agreed to sit for Robert and no other sculptor.

Bronze statues (left) by Robert Thomas called 'Independence' (foreground) and 'Reflection', (background), with 'Girl' (opposite page) all situated in front of Tŷ Crawshay, University of South Wales

In the last twelve years of his life (Robert died in 1999), he produced a set of statues specifically for Wales: the landmark Aneurin Bevan statue in Queen Street, Cardiff and the imaginary 'Captain Cat' from Dylan Thomas's Under Milk Wood in Swansea. Robert added a third to this series; the well-loved Miner's Family Group' for Llwynypia in the Rhondda which stands on the site of the Tonypandy Riots of 1910 and 1911.

The University is blessed with five works by Robert Thomas: three statues from his "free figure" series and two portrait busts from his "Welsh contemporaries" series. The statues are located, appropriately, in the garden outside the building in which he studied. They are 'Girl' and 'Independence' (both on long-term loan from the Derek Williams Trust) and 'Reflection' (which is owned by the University). The busts are of two eminent sons of south Wales miners: Aneurin Bevan (displayed in the Aneurin Bevan building, Glyntaf, and unveiled by the First Minister Rhodri Morgan in April 2007) and Roderick Jones, the Ferndale-born opera singer (donated to the University by his widow).

Both Robert Thomas and Alan Holloway had happy outcomes to their war experiences. Some didn't end as happily, such as the story of part-time student William Ivor Wright.

Ivor lived at 79 Regent Street, Treorchy, and worked as an Assistant Surveyor for the Ocean Coal Company. He had begun his part-time Surveying Course in September 1939 and he passed easily into the second year. Like many students, Ivor took on extra activities and responsibilities when war broke out – he joined his local battalion of the Home Guard: the 7th Glamorganshire (Pentre) Battalion. The Rhondda area hadn't been greatly troubled by enemy action, but on the night of Tuesday, April 29th 1941, the Cwmparc area of Treorchy was unexpectedly bombed by the Luftwaffe (the German Air Force). It isn't understood why the area was suddenly hit in such a devastating way; it may be that the bomber was jettisoning unused bombs whilst making a home run after targeting Swansea or Cardiff. But the effect on Cwmparc was horrific and tragic. It's likely the bombs were incendiaries and high explosive devices and they ripped through the village – the focus of the damage was Treharne Street and Parc Road. It was reported that Ivor saw one of these devices falling, suspended from a parachute which he may have believed was a German or British airman.

As a Home Guard soldier, he rushed to investigate but the device exploded and he was killed instantly. He was just 19 years of age.

26 other people died that night including, tragically, three children who had been evacuated from another area more likely to be affected by enemy action.

Ivor's loss was sorely felt by fellow students at the School of Mines and Technology, but they did him proud at his funeral – the students' annual publication, Breccia, of 1941-42 carries an account:

"The [Officer] Cadet Corps, at the request of the Student Representative Council, represented the School of Mines at the funeral of the late Ivor Wright (Home Guard), a part-time student, who was killed by enemy action in Cwmparc. About 20 cadets turned up at Treorchy, and their performance, both during and after the funeral, was more than a credit to the Corps. Tea was afterwards provided by the Treorchy Home Guard, and a letter of thanks was received by our O.C. [Officer in Charge]"

The bombed area of Cwmparc has never been redeveloped and grass now grows over the lumps and bumps of wrecked homes, neatly softening the outlines of the tragedy of 1941.

Above: The site today of the bombing of Cwmparc in 1941. This event was witnessed by Robert Thomas and also his fellow part time student William Ivor Wright

FOUNDRY CLASS, SCHOOL OF MINES AND TECHNOLOGY, TREFOREST.

APRIL 19th, 1941.

Back Row—G. Davies, G. Rees, D. Morgan, F. Davies, W. K. Davies, D. Steele, J. R. Jones, A. Sullock, N. Gardener, G. Ashford, D. Gardener, R. Sealey, W. E. Davies, M. Lynch, G. Aubrey.

4th Row—W. A. Rowbotham, J. Morgan, G. Palfrey, D. Gaze, C. H. Miller, W. Gould, A. H. Cannard, E. J. Bailey, K. Davies, E. Pate, G. Nicholas, H. Smith, E. Coombes.

3rd Row—W. Kinsman, W. Thomas, L. Biddiscombe, W. Hughes, G. Kinglake, G. May, M. James, W. Morgan, H. Miles, M. Hanks, J. Lott, R. Gittins, R. Green, W. Tomkins, J. Sime, J. A. Williams.

2nd Row—J. Williams, S. Protheroe, F. J. Gist, R. Metcalfe, A. Pearson, M.P., C. E. Williams, J.P., R. J. Richardson, Prin. R. James, P. Jacobs, Dr. W. R. D. Jones, Mr. Corney, B. E. Lewis, H. Lenox, E. J. Kelly

Front Row—D. McCarthy, P. Farr, J. Evans, I. Jones, M. Richards, L. Tarr, W. Thomas, O. Greenway, W. Oakley.

Acknowledged or not, there are always gains from war and, arguably, the School of Mines and Technology gained in a number of ways. In a report of July 1940 written by Principal James, it's clear that a considerable amount of war-related work came the way of the School – with an efficient production line operating from the workshops:

"The contract work in hand embraces jobs for the Admiralty, an Explosives Works, and an Aluminium Factory.

Following negotiations with the firms concerned, prices per unit article produced have been agreed. As typical figures, one may mention a contract for turning 600 brass bushes at 1/1½ each, and another for 3,000 copper ferrules at 1/6 per gross. The production work at Treforest is being carried out by the Workshop Mechanics, and by members of the teaching staff, ex-members of the staff like Mr Firth, and one or two voluntary workers, in the evening."

Above: The School's Foundry class of 1941

T. H. THOMAS
President of the Students' Representative Council, 1941–1942.

Everyone who made widgets (which probably ended up in aircraft, munitions, or other wartime essentials) did so voluntarily and the most they received by way of payment was a contribution toward their travelling expenses. The profit after expenses was banked by the Glamorganshire County Council! What's more – the School's summer shut-down was cancelled from summer 1940 onward, with staff being offered a reduced 10 days or a fortnight's holiday!

Students gained from the opportunity to join the Home Guard or the Officer Cadet Corps. The Corps (after its initial application was turned down) was working well by November 1940, generating 'intense interest' from the students. It was set up under the command of 'Fuels' lecturer Mr Sid Watkins, who reached the rank of Colonel by the end of the war. Even from its earliest days, the Corps was 60 students strong and Principal James was very proud of this activity as he reported to the Management Committee that the students *"have been devoting their Saturday afternoon to route-marching, signalling, lectures on map-reading etc... and when the Corps parades in uniform, they will undoubtedly reflect credit on the School."* And so they did.

The curriculum gained breadth by expanding in specialist areas to meet the requests of the War Office. There were numerous examples – a Foundry Practice Course started in December 1940 with 80 students paying a fee of 3/- each. The class ran between 12.30 and 2.00 pm on a Saturday afternoon

and its success was largely down to Mr Richardson, the Manager of Brown Lennox and Co, Pontypridd who gave over a portion of the foundry for use by the class. If it hadn't been for this generous arrangement, the course may have stalled since the workshop space available at Treforest was under severe strain by this time.

Another major influx of student soldiers arrived to take the Wireless Mechanics course which was designed at the request of the Ministry. This was a bit more problematic for the School as it didn't have expertise in this kind of electrical engineering; the inside of a wireless being a long way removed from the heavy engineering needed for the mining industry. The School brought in two staff to teach the course and the workload was pretty tough: teaching was 44 ½ hours each week for 16 weeks and as soon as one large group passed out to join their military units then

Above: T. H. Thomas, President of the Students' Representative Council, 1941-1942

Right: Advert showing colliery equipment made and supplied by Brown Lenox & Co, Treforest. The company were also admiralty contractors and reputedly made the anchor chain for the Titanic

another group started immediately. There was also a bit of a worry that the School didn't have the right equipment for students to learn with – the War Office had promised to supply the *'right apparatus and wireless valves'* but when it didn't show up the School rented kit owned by Mr R. H. James, one of the course's new teachers.

An unexpected addition to the student numbers came from Swansea Technical College (now part of Swansea Metropolitan University). The College had also developed new courses to meet war requirements and one of these was a 16 week course training Turners (a skilled craft turning metal or wood on a lathe). Swansea, because of its importance as a port, had been subject to attacks by the Luftwaffe from 1940 onward, but over three nights in February 1941 the city was the focus of a sustained blitz which left areas of the centre (but not the docks or industrial areas) in ashes and rubble. It was the most devastating attack on any city outside London with between 800 and 900 properties destroyed and thousands damaged. One of the damaged buildings was the College – and the students were only half-way through their course. As desperately overcrowded as the Treforest School was at the time, the Principal agreed to take 10 students to finish their course in Treforest. All student soldiers were billeted in the surrounding area as the School had no hostel of its own at the time.

In addition to the metaphorical regiments of student soldiers at the

The devastating results of the three nights blitz on Swansea's High Street and College Street, above, and Castle Street, opposite

ROYAL ENGINEERS CADET CORPS
Affiliated to
588th (GLAM.) ARMY TROOP COMPANY, R.E.
CERTIFICATE " A " SQUAD.

School, the number of civilian students also increased steadily. This, although welcomed, brought with it more headaches about lack of space. For example, in 1942-43, 709 students enrolled compared with 570 from the year before. Thankfully, the School managed to get some extra teaching accommodation, however the pressure on space was so acute that the Principal managed to convince the County Council to build a 'hut' as a matter of urgency. 'Hut' was the description the School applied to it, but it was probably very comfortable and well-fitted as huts go. Mr James had asked for an 'Army hut' of some 60 by 20 feet, but this proved to be unobtainable as the materials they were made from were subject to special war-time licenses.

Instead, a much more glamorous 'hut' was built from a material called Maycrete (a type of pre-cast concrete panel) which could be bolted together quickly. This building was an expensive option as it cost £1,420, but it was undoubtedly exceptional value for money given that it existed until around 1980 and in post-war years housed the Student Services Department and, later, a research laboratory. Another part solution to the space problem was found by renting the Treforest Boys Club building on Queen Street. In true make-do-and-mend fashion the building was 'converted' into a state-of-the-art teaching room by painting a wall with blackboard paint!

Above: The Royal Engineers Cadet Corps at the School of Mines

Left: During the three nights blitz a massive number of incendiary bombs were dropped on the city with the resulting fires gutting most buildings that were not damaged by explosives. St Mary's Church is visible in this photograph with its tower remaining, but the roof and interior gutted

Mechanical Engineering Laboratory

Physics Laboratory

Surveying Drawing Office

With the benefit of hindsight, the overcrowded wartime classrooms were just a rehearsal for things to come in the post-war years. From September 1946 (the first full academic year after the end of the war) many students who had been away on service returned to study with 1,145 students enrolling that year requiring innovative, and sometimes unconventional solutions to the space problem! Further challenging growth was to come, but this was eventually accompanied by a building programme to match.

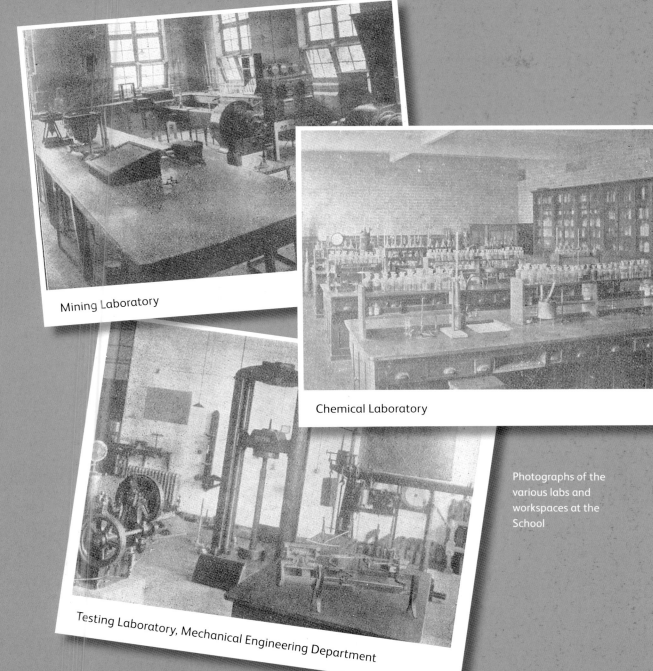

Mining Laboratory

Chemical Laboratory

Testing Laboratory, Mechanical Engineering Department

Photographs of the various labs and workspaces at the School

127

ENGINEERING CADETS

Front Row : A. Carr,   L. Hardy   J. Lloyd   W. D. Walters (Pres.),   C. Smale,   G. T. Phillips,   J. Chapman
Second Row : J. Miles,   L. Smith,   L. Bond   W. Williams,   J. D. Brown
Third Row : R. Dale,   S. Jones,   P. John   K. Anthoney,   R. Cox,   I. Harris
Fourth Row : R. Pritchard,   L. Harris   E. J. Morgan

The Second World War was such a busy, interesting and challenging time for the School and its students that it's sad to omit stories which have never been told. Stories such as Mr Stone, the caretaker-cum-librarian, and his ARP (Air Raid Precaution) duties; the story of fire-watchers on camp beds with stirrup pump to hand to save the building; the story of the old Barry Railway line (now a campus car park) being used to 'park' American machinery of war for the D-Day landings; the story of the gift of an old armoured car to the Home Guard and Cadet Corps at the School; the story of students travelling to evening classes in blackout conditions. And, most of all, the story of all the students who left their studies to serve in the forces and of those who returned and those

who didn't. All of this is aching to be told, but the records leave one with the clear impression that all characters in the story were proud of what they did to meet the needs of the war effort. It feels as if they enjoyed it; that they maintained a sense of fun during the serious times and that there was a great feeling of camaraderie – of pulling together.

The School grew up during these years and it is no coincidence that it's at this point that the wearisome discussions about its possible status as a department of the University College, Cardiff, faded away. The School had earned the right to its existence – it was here to stay.

Above: The Schools Engineering Cadets

Left: Blackout Blues', a cartoon featured in the 1939-40 Breccia making light of the Blackout rules during the Second World War

CHAPTER 4
The turbulent Seventies

The "Poly" days

The challenges faced in the post war years – achieving a lot with a little and coping with the inward rush of new students full of high hopes – turned out to be just a rehearsal for the years to come. The 1950s and '60s saw steady growth in both curriculum and campus accommodation. A White Paper entitled *Technical Education* of 1956 had designated Glamorgan Technical College as a 'Regional College' which warranted a change of name; and so

it was that The Glamorgan College of Technology came into being in 1958. Then, in 1960, the relocation of non-advanced vocational courses to the new Further Education College in Rhydyfelin (today Coleg Morgannwg) left Treforest with a portfolio of almost entirely advanced courses. And in 1963, the College's golden jubilee year, a large new building housing an extensive library, high tech workshops and laboratories, and a large hall was

Above: On 1 August 2013 Coleg Y Cymoedd (formerly Pontypridd College and, earlier, the Further Education College Rhydyfelin) at Nantgarw was offically opened. This was due to the merger between Coleg Morgannwg and The College, Ystrad Mynach

[1] Dominic Sandbrook, Blog in The Guardian, on-line, 16th April 2012,
http://www.guardian.co.uk/tv-and-radio/tvandradioblog/2012/apr/16/the-70s-bbc2.

"No decade in recent memory has had a worse press than the Seventies. In our collective memory, these were years of strikes and blackouts, financial crises and terrorist atrocities, terrible wallpaper and undrinkable wine" [1]

opened. Of all these advances, the new status as a 'Regional' College was of the greatest significance since it was largely institutions with this status which went on to become the Polytechnics of the 1970s.

Contemporary historian Dominic Sandbrook has written of the seventies that "No decade in recent memory has had a worse press than the Seventies. In our collective memory, these were years of strikes and blackouts, financial crises and terrorist atrocities, terrible wallpaper and undrinkable wine" [1]

One might add a few more things. It was pretty normal to discriminate against women – in 1970 working women in the UK were refused mortgages in their own right and were only granted mortgages if they could obtain the signature of a male guarantor. And it was as late as 1975 that the Sex Discrimination Act was passed making it illegal to discriminate against women in work, education and training. Similarly if you were black or of an ethnic minority, you would have to wait until 1976 for the Race Relations Act to make discrimination in employment and education illegal. Yet however bleak that seems, it is far from the whole story as a historic opportunity was on the horizon for the Glamorgan College of Technology.

National politics, local impacts

The opportunity offered to the College originated in the autumn of 1963 when Lord Robbins' Committee on Higher Education published its report. The Committee had been appointed by the Conservative Government under Prime Minister Harold Macmillan *'to review the pattern of full-time higher education in Great Britain and in the light of national needs and resources to advise….on what principles its long-term development should be based. In particular….whether there should be any changes in that pattern, whether any new types of institution are desirable…'* Robbins concluded that *"…the system should provide for those who had the qualifications and the willingness to pursue higher education,"* [2] by which he meant that students should be supported to study through grants and the payments of fees. The recommendations meant existing universities should expand and Colleges of Advanced Technology (one level above the Glamorgan College of Technology) should take on the status and powers of universities. Most of the reports recommendations were implemented, including the hike in the number of institutions, but parts of the plan were handled through a different means: the establishment of Polytechnics.

At Treforest, the first indication that Polytechnic status was likely came in a letter in April 1967 to Glamorgan County Council's Director of Education. It was sent from the Education Officer for Wales, of the Department of Education and Science and invited *"…the Authority to submit a scheme for the establishment of a Polytechnic".* This letter speaks prophetically of *"…the part which they will play in the future development of higher education alongside the universities and the colleges of education, great importance attaches to the establishment of the Polytechnics".* Treforest was the only institution in Wales to be among the 28 planned polytechnics on the original list issued by the Secretary of State (two more were added soon after). The County Council had been provided with guidelines and these included some 'expectations' of the future Poly. For example, it would have to have *'the potential for ultimate growth to at least 2,000 full-time students plus part-time students from the Polytechnic's catchment area'.* No problem there, then.

[2] Report of the Committee appointed by the Prime Minister under the Chairmanship of Lord Robbins 1961-63, LONDON, HMSO.

Planning for a
Polytechnic

A special sub-committee was set up to think through the 'impending developments', although interestingly (and amusingly) this enormously significant work was passed to the group along with the job of looking at staff levels needed in a new student hostel! It now seems odd that two such diverse plans were being worked on by the same small group at the same time. But perhaps it's not that odd. The County Council couldn't have foreseen the enormous long term potential of Polytechnics, and the planned 100-bed student hostel was a massive undertaking as it brought a large expansion of the College's workforce: a Housekeeper/Nurse and an assistant, a full-time maid, 15 part-time maids, a porter, a night watchman and a boilerman.

By August 1967 plans for Polytechnic status were coming together: the new hostel was completed and named 'Forest Hall'. Other staffing levels hadn't been increased since 1959 and needed urgent attention. Additional support staff: a Switchboard Operator and Duplicating Operator, a Maintenance Operator and extra porters, plus cleaning staff were all put in place. There were other major investments: the library's book fund had a substantial injection of cash, more staff were recruited to the library and to the body of technicians. Norman Morris, in 2013 the University's longest serving staff member, recalls the extent of the changes needed for Polytechnic status and he refers to it as the biggest wave of change he can recall in his 50 years service.

On the academic side, there were a few glitches to overcome. The Council for National Academic Awards (CNAA) had been set up in 1964 to approve the standard of degrees from non-university institutions. The College of Technology's degree in Civil Engineering had been turned down for approval and this was a major blow. The problem was largely the 'academic structure'; there were not enough highly qualified staff and the College was advised to move rapidly towards the arrangements for staff and academic departments expected for the new Polytechnics. The honours degree in Chemical Engineering had been approved, but this too had come with a strong steer about staffing and organisation of academic departments. As a result, a new department of Chemical Engineering was set up under the leadership of Gwilym Bolan, who was himself a graduate of the School of Mines from the Second World War years.

On equal terms

To become a Polytechnic the work was daunting, the re-organisation testing, and the costs eye-watering. But Polys were seen as a key factor in the long-term economic prosperity of the UK – so Glamorgan County Council stepped up to the mark and made it so. Glamorgan Polytechnic was created on 1st April 1970 and its official document of designation was signed later in the year by Margaret Thatcher, Secretary of State for Education and Science following the general election. The Polys went on to become remarkably successful at what they did: they designed and delivered modern, applied courses fit for a growing range of professions and industry. The Poly experience was less about learning for the intrinsic worth of acquiring knowledge, and more about learning with an end application in mind – as had been the original modus operandi of the School of Mines. At the same time the Polys attracted a more diverse student body than the traditional, 'old' universities – particularly noticeable were those who were the first of their family line to enter higher education, part-time students, and mature students returning to study. Polytechnics were so good at their particular brand of higher education that it has been said that they 'went on to transform higher education in the next quarter century'.[3]

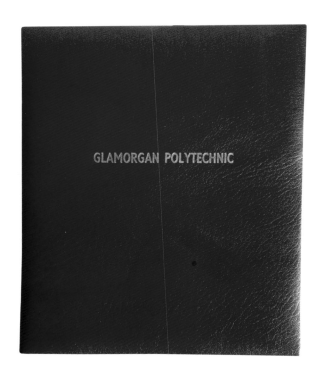

Above, right: The official document designating Glamorgan Polytechnic, signed by Margaret Thatcher

[3] John Pratt, Times Higher Education, 1997

GLAMORGAN POLYTECHNIC

This INSTRUMENT
records the designation of this
Institution as a Polytechnic on
1st April 1970.
In commemoration of this,
on behalf of Her Majesty's
Government, I hereby set my seal.

Secretary of State for Education and Science

Courses
and campuses

The curriculum had already started to change. The passing decades had diminished mining and many new, varied industries offered alternative employment. For example, a non-profit making company had created Treforest Industrial Estate in 1936 with three small factories, and its aim was to provide alternative employment to those traditional industries which were now in decline. The modern, emerging industries required a different range of skills and qualifications of their employees and the curriculum adapted and expanded to meet that need. The 1970-71 prospectus reflected this change, although it still had a strong paternalistic air about it; for example, students were firmly instructed that drawing pins were not allowed in the Engineering Drawing room! However, alongside the long-standing range of engineering subjects, there now appeared the likes of Management Studies, Modern Foreign Languages, Business Studies, Computer Programming, Chartered Accountants and Urban Estate Management.

The staff mix started to change along with the curriculum: 8 women teaching staff were employed in 1970-71, alongside the 180 men; a ratio of around 22 to 1. The broader range of courses started to attract students from a wider geographic area than the Glamorgan coalfield; students in that year were drawn from Dunvant to Damascus and most points in between, although those from outside the coalfield areas were still in the minority. Numbers of women students had started to increase slowly – arguably a welcome improvement in such a male dominated environment! Women had begun to arrive in extremely small numbers as early as 1941, and for the next couple of decades the numbers remained almost invisible. But by 1971 the number had risen to 57, yet they still had to contend with a male/female ratio of around 13:1, no college accommodation (Forest Hall was strictly male only), and some pretty traditional attitudes. For example, the prospectus advertised summer craft courses to be held in late July and August with 'Crafts for Women' on offer: dressmaking, embroidery, soft furnishings, cookery, millinery, and floral decoration.

The campus too was changing rapidly. Indeed, although important building work had been undertaken during the sixties (B Block and Forest Hall), from 1970 onward for the whole decade, one major building project or another was on the go. There's no other way to describe the campus other than 'grim on times'. In June 1970 the current Glynneath building (G Block) was started, to house the Department of Civil Engineering and Building. Later that same year, building work began on the Hirwaun building

Right: Treforest Industrial estate 2013

Below: Construction begins on the Polytechnic 1970

(H Block), which was to be the home of the Department of Business Studies. In late 1972 the first Students' Union building was opened, to be followed shortly by the first phase of the Library, the Upper Refectory (now Stilts Restaurant), and another hall of residence (Phillip Evans Hall). From 1976, work began on Johnstown and Dyffryn buildings (J Block and D Block).

The prospectus optimistically says

"During the next ten years or so, it is hoped that the master plan will be completed...."

The students must have fervently hoped so, too.

Although if the campus concrete mixers were tiresome, then perhaps the site's sheep population provided a little amusement, or puzzlement at least! On occasions, the campus hosted more than sheep when a local farmer, presumably a man who had skipped the class on building and maintaining fences, allowed livestock to roam across the campus, and Treforest in general! Early morning cleaners would take a break, tea in hand, to watch lambs being born on the grass between 'B Block' and Llantwit Road. The grassy stretch between the library and Central Avenue, now where the extended library building is, was often home to cows, and even the occasional pig would roam the campus and raid the bins of Treforest's householders. The farmer would occasionally turn up on campus, sometimes on horseback, to round up these animals. On other times he would arrive in a long wheelbase Land Rover, complete with sheepdog in the back, and staff and students would be treated to a demonstration of rounding up sheep – a number of which would be hauled into the back of the Land Rover and given a lift home – until next time.

Above: Brecon Building 1963

Left: Further construction on the Polytechnic 1970

Student life

It is a blessing that most students from the early Poly years are still around and able to contribute recollections to this book – although most would prefer not to recall the tank-tops, bell bottoms and similar fashion must-haves, or that the seventies was probably the golden age of the moustache! A prominent student of the decade, complete with moustache, was Student Union president of 1974, Graham Pitcher. Graham was, as a student, symbolic of the changing student body. He was not working in the mining industry and not a local man, but a Londoner. He also neatly represents the seventies in that he first enrolled on the BSc Chemical Engineering course in 1970 when employed as an undergraduate apprentice by BP at Llandarcy. He was elected President of the Students' Union in 1974, left to work for GKN in Cardiff, and returned to complete his degree, graduating at the close of the decade.

Graham recollects that in the early years of the decade the Students' Union was a pretty 'loose' organisation *'with a president, secretary and a couple of other named positions, but it wasn't what you would call an active organisation'*. The physical space for the Union, until the new building was completed, amounted to a common room just off the stairs opposite the lower refectory in B block. It was equipped with seats and a table football machine, but had no beer, no music and little attraction. In terms of political activities, one might have expected that in the era of the Three-day Week (as Prime Minister Edward Heath tried to control the power of the trade unions) the Students' Union would have seen a lot of political activity. But commitment to action wasn't simple for this 'junior' organisation since the majority of students were still part-time and, although probably politically active, that activity would have been through their

Left: Graham Pitcher, Students' Union President (1974) then and now

Above: Cartoon from the Students' Union handbook

Right: Hefin Wyn Edwards, Students' Union President (1977-78)

'Great news, your grant cheque has arrived!'

own trade union or local politics rather than the student body.

However, the Union was learning to find its political feet. Members raised issues at Poly level and took part in local and national activities through NUS conferences. In March 1975, Graham Pitcher recalls South Wales students giving United States Secretary of State Henry Kissinger a 'warm welcome' when he arrived in Cardiff to attend a banquet in honour of James Callaghan. The student representatives were beginning to take issues to the Poly's Director, Dr. D.W.F (Francis) James, an example of which was an early demand for more prominence for the Welsh language. In 1975 the Union had a minor clash with Dr James over a visit from Reg Prentice, Secretary of State for Education under the Labour Prime Minister Harold Wilson. The Director had required 'no trouble' from the Students' Union, but the President took the opportunity to

'button hole' Mr. Prentice and hand him a letter setting out students' objections to cutbacks. Dr. James was not impressed.

The Union received a *per capita* grant from the Poly and used it to fund clubs and societies. It also produced a student newspaper called *Yr Aurlas* (reflecting the Poly colours of blue and gold) and this, together with the Union's handbook, is a time capsule of student life and attitudes of the day. It covered politics, music, the social scene and risqué 'page three' style photographs of women alongside advice on how to spot the symptoms of sexually transmitted diseases.

Dr. James was an interesting character: a man of high chapel-like principles and standards, serious in nature, paternalistic towards students, deeply caring towards staff and a fighter for his institution. But a father figure,

"I THOUGHT THE GUY MEANT **BOB** DYLAN!"

whether in the shape of Dr. James or the institution, in its proprietorial relationship with the Union, was not what students wanted or expected by the mid-seventies. Graham Pitcher recalls *"…we installed a condom machine in the new Students Union building. Dr. James was not amused and ordered it not to be used. His view was that such a move would require the approval of the Governing Body. Needless to say, we weren't amused either. I attended the meeting, all ready to justify the move. As the item came up on the agenda, the good old tea lady arrived with coffee: Dr. James refused to let the discussion proceed until she had left the room. Then the Chairman said "Does anyone have any objections?" No hands were raised and the machine was filled up again. It was another world"*.

The question of independence of the Union (students would have described it as 'interference') was contentious in other ways. For example, the Secretary and Clerk to the Governors, Peter Gillibrand, was the legal licensee for the bar, meaning the Poly had to approve late licenses for events. The Poly also retained a seat on the Union's Executive Board and took a steer in key Union appointments. A major stand-off between the Union's Executive and the Poly came about through one particular appointment. A new post of Administrator was of singular importance to the Union for business, organisation of events, management of its membership and so on. The post was advertised, interviews conducted and, as a result of the Poly's influence, it was offered to and accepted by a member of the Finance Department's staff. But the Union's Executive felt the appointment to be a 'plant' and the decision was thrown out; this was a step too far. The eventual appointment of an independent person helped to embed the feelings of effective independence for the Students' Union.

Above: Cartoon from the Students Union handbook

With a growing number of students living in Forest Hall or in local digs, a range of social activities was very important. However, these had to be almost completely created by students for students, since Treforest and Pontypridd were not overly edowed with options and venturing to Cardiff was almost unheard of for a night out. The *White Hart* in Pontypridd was regarded as THE place to go for a pub session, and a trip to the town's single Chinese restaurant was a high spot. The pubs in Treforest were assured of good levels of custom: *The Commercial* (later to be renamed '*The Otley Arms*'), *The Crown* and *The Rickard's Arms* being the more usual destinations. Students would organise occasional events in Pontypridd with the aim of boosting the Union's coffers, but these didn't always go according to plan: around 1974 the Union organised a gig with a band called 'Kenny' featuring Keith Chegwin. It was hoped many local youngsters

would turn up, but they had more sense and the Union's bank balance took the hit. Much better luck was had with gigs in the main hall in B Block (known until recently as B12) with the 'essential' bar being located downstairs in the lower refectory. Featured at these gigs and recalled by Graham were: Roy Wood and Wizzard, Spencer Davies, Heavy Metal Kids, Babe Ruth and The Troggs among others. The Troggs gig in particular was a memorable evening – for the wrong reasons! It was a time when the band's lead singer, Reg Presley, had some personal health issues. The band had played a couple of songs when Presley suddenly disappeared off the stage. Some band members shortly followed to see if they could find him, leaving just the drummer facing the audience. The search revealed that Presley had gone into the downstairs dressing rooms, climbed out of the window and disappeared into the night!

Above: Otley Arms

Left: The Troggs, who played a memorable show in the main hall of B Block

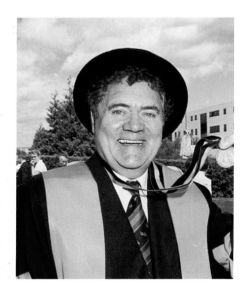

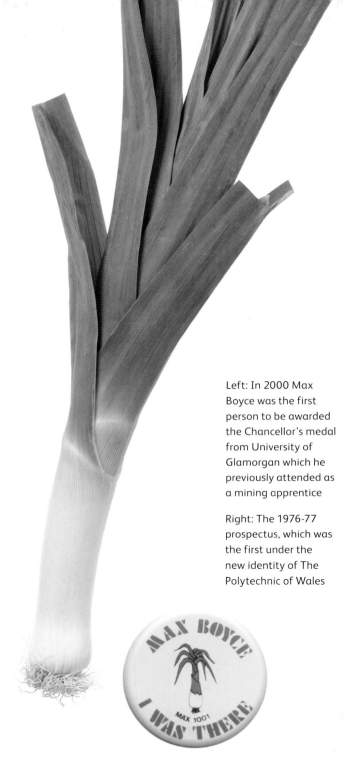

In addition to such highlights, the Union building was occasionally used for an evening event, for example, the Folk Club. These events were 'lubricated' by the Union's 10 pence per pint policy (set by the Executive so students could get a good night out for 50 pence). Max Boyce (himself a former student of Mining) performed at the Folk Club and Graham Pitcher recalls that Max picked up a giant leek 'prop' which had been lying around the Union and used it that evening – so perhaps the Glamorgan Poly Union had inadvertently provided Max's trademark 'badge' which he was then to use for some years to come!

Left: In 2000 Max Boyce was the first person to be awarded the Chancellor's medal from University of Glamorgan which he previously attended as a mining apprentice

Right: The 1976-77 prospectus, which was the first under the new identity of The Polytechnic of Wales

THE POLYTECHNIC OF WALES
Politechnig Cymru
Prospectus of Full-time
& Sandwich Courses
1976-77

This is the first publication of our Full-time Prospectus following the merger of the Glamorgan College of Education with the Glamorgan Polytechnic. The new enlarged institution has been designated **The Polytechnic of Wales.** The establishment of our new status gives formal recognition to the position of the only Polytechnic in Wales, allowing further emphasis to our regional and national role

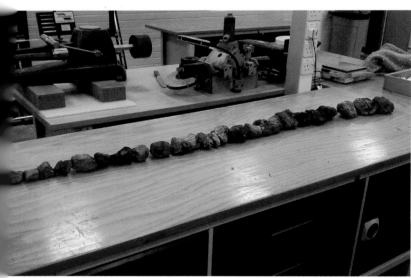

Above: The remains of the Iguanodon tail found by the Polytechnic students in 1975

Most of the Poly's full-time courses at the time had 'sandwich placements' built in; that is, practical periods in industry or commerce as in the original School of Mines model. This meant that after Easter the campus went quiet, as only part-time students remained whilst full-time students went off to employment. Another sizeable group of students left the campus around Easter for a long-standing annual 'jolly' to the Isle of Wight: the famous Geology and Surveying Field Trip. This trip, still organised by the University after almost 50 years, involved up to 150 to 200 students taking up residence on the island at a holiday camp near Sandown. In the Seventies, the course leader was the well-respected geologist (and writer on the history of the Poly) Basil Isaac. Many stories, some best not repeated, were generated from this field trip. One story stands out: the discovery of the dinosaur!

Early in May 1975 the usual large party of students took the two week course and they examined a clay bed which had been a river delta some 120 million years ago. A second year student, Martin Hutchinson, uncovered a number of vertebrae which were provisionally identified by the staff as an 'Iguanodon'. The discovery diverted the planned schedule for the course as teams of students continued the excavations, and this exciting find was confirmed as a rare event by the Curator of the Isle of Wight's geological museum. Basil Isaac wrote *'After much digging it was found that the tail was not attached to the rest of the skeleton…the remainder of the skeleton is probably in the cliff'*. The Curator's inside information that a well-known American university was paying large sums for Isle of Wight dinosaur fossils was a spur to the field course the following year!

Spirits were no doubt running high in the year of the dinosaur find as another story runs about a practical joke played on one ultra-keen student. His colleagues had secured a large beef shoulder bone from a local butcher's, and 'planted' it in the earth where it was sure to be 'discovered'. It was; and amid great excitement it was scientifically classified by the good sport Basil Isaac as *'Bos Dewhurstii'* – Bos being the generic name of an ancient, extinct cow, and 'Dewhurst' being a well known chain of butchers' stores! The real dinosaur's tail was eventually identified by the Natural History Museum, London, as Iguanodon Bernissartensis;

a vegetarian beast over 15 feet tall, with impressive spiked spurs on its front legs. It was cleaned, preserved, mounted and displayed for many years in the entrance to the Glynneath building and remains in the building to this day.

Archaeologist's impressions of the Iguanodon

The first merger
and 'Hello Poly'

If Glamorgan Poly's students were largely preoccupied with their studies, social life, sex and dinosaur discoveries, then staff were concerned with major strategic decisions which dominated the middle years of the decade.

The first of these was the introduction of a major new arts degree in 1973: the BA Humanities – offering students the option to combine subjects such as Philosophy, Geography, History, English, Religious Studies and others. The degree had two effects: it brought with it more women staff and students, and it started a move towards more balance in the Poly's curriculum between engineering and the arts.

The second major change was the Poly's merger with Glamorgan College of Education; the teacher training college based at Barry in the (then) South Glamorgan county area. A merger of colleges is a big event, as students and staff of the University of Glamorgan in 2013 are well aware. So what was the reason for the 1970s merger and what happened to the other college? It's not an unfamiliar story: it concerns government policy in difficult financial times and pinched public sector budgets.

At the time, it was not the Welsh Government in Cardiff Bay which dictated education policy. The (then) un-trendy bay area was still black with small coal, disused docks and home to some of Cardiff's poorer housing. Education policy and government budgets were set by the UK government in London, and Edward Heath's Conservative government, which had been running the country since June 1970, had a problem. The Conservatives had a House of Commons majority of just 30 seats but it needed to push through policies to tackle worryingly high inflation rates. One means of doing this was through cuts in public expenditure. For example, Heath's Secretary of State for Education, Margaret Thatcher, helpfully identified one cost-saving measure – the end of the universal provision of free milk for school children, earning herself the nickname of 'Thatcher the Milk Snatcher' in the process.

The need for tightened budgets was combined with a falling birth-rate, which meant smaller school rolls and smaller teams to teach them. However, teachers were still being churned out by the many training colleges, and too few graduates were finding jobs. The Government's solution to this was the reorganisation of teacher training colleges and the plan was set out in a 1972 White Paper *Education: A Framework for Expansion*. It required lower numbers of students entering teacher training and demanded that the smaller training colleges formed 'closer associations' with other institutions or broadened their range of courses (although this latter option would be difficult if the college was in close proximity to a sizeable institution with a broad offering of its own).

The numbers speak for themselves. In Wales, teacher training was offered at nine different colleges; six in South Wales and three in North Wales. The cities of Cardiff and Bangor had two teacher training colleges each! Like it or not, merger would be a cost saver and just plain common sense. So, following a rash of working parties and sub-committees, Glamorgan College of Education and the Poly merged in 1975. The newly enlarged institution was recognised by a change of name: The Polytechnic of Wales. The new name also reflected that the 'Poly' was the only one of its kind in Wales, and would always be so.

So there it is, in 1975 the Polytechnic of Wales had two campuses some 15 miles apart, and the expansion was warmly welcomed. These positive feelings come through in staff publications such as *The Gazette* of 1974-75 which, with more enthusiasm than élan, included a 'home-made' variation of a well-known film theme song:

'Hullo Poly! Well Hullo Poly!
It's so nice to be right in where we belong.
We're all so swell, Poly,
We can tell, Poly,
We're now glowing and we're growing
And we'll keep going strong.
We feel the world swaying and the band's playing
One of those old Celtic songs from way back when;
So – Poly Wales – fellas,
Grab yourself some new degrees fellas,
Oh Poly, don't break away again!'

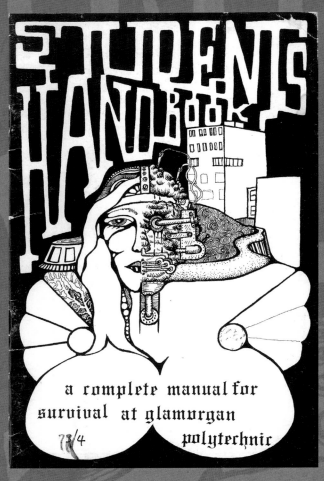

Students' handbooks

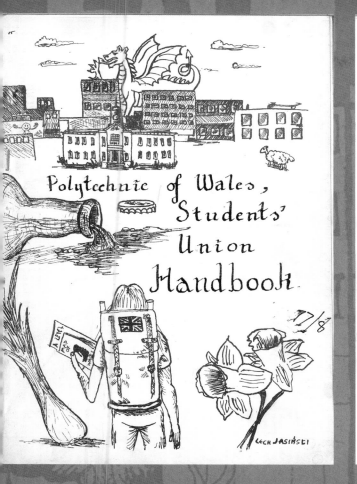

However, by 1981, just six years later, the Barry campus would be closed and teacher training ended. This really sounds like the most cavalier approach to strategic planning and the lives of staff and students, but these were strangely testing times.

It isn't easy to briefly summarise what happened, but the British economy was in a very precarious position. The country had experienced a quadrupling of oil prices and the knock-on effect on the costs of goods and services resulted in enormous inflation rates – the crisis was so bad that the Government even issued petrol ration books! Workers, in turn, demanded higher pay awards to keep pace with the cost of living, but Edward Heath's administration had imposed an incomes policy to restrict these claims. Lengthy confrontations with powerful trade unions followed: rubbish lay in the streets and the dead remained unburied. Most notably among the pugilistic unions was the National Union of Miners (the NUM), which challenged Heath again and again. In 1974, Mr. Heath called a general election, asking the question "Who governs Britain?" (meaning the elected government or influential trades unions, particularly the NUM).

The answer to the question was NOT Edward Heath. The election was lost, but the difficulties didn't disappear after the votes were counted. By the spring of 1975, in the time of Harold Wilson's Labour government, unemployment had climbed to around a million – over 5% of the workforce – and the strain on the public purse was acute. Among the sad ranks of the unemployed were far too many teachers – the mergers and cuts in student places hadn't achieved enough.

The decision was made: the Polytechnic of Wales would end its entire teacher training courses by the summer of 1981. The government's cuts initially

Left to right: Students' Union presidents from the 70s: Alan Harris (71-72); Pat Riley (73-74); Tim Collins (76-77); Alun Pugh (78-79); Julian Hamilton Fisher (79-80)

Below: A cartoon from the Students' Union Handbook reflecting worries about employment prospects

155

"This is Pugh — studying engineering, design and hoping for the Duke of Edinburgh Award."

meant that *two* South Wales' colleges would lose their teacher training, the Poly and West Glamorgan Institute of Higher Education (now Swansea Metropolitan University). But following mighty political manoeuvring and high level discussions, the West Glamorgan Institute was reprieved. Dr. James was incensed and fought to save his courses and save his staff jobs. He said, in an interview for the Times Higher Educational Supplement in July 1977 *"I am absolutely disgusted that the Government has refused to change its mind….this is a straight political decision"*. He felt the decision had been based on Welsh language considerations in that the Poly graduates were trained only for teaching through the medium of English. He also felt strongly that the Poly was a victim of its own success at diversifying its curriculum which *"… encouraged people to believe it could survive without teacher training."* Without doubt he was right, but as much as he and the Poly's trade unions objected the authorities were not persuaded – it hadn't lasted long but this was the end of the road for teacher training.

On the brighter side, Mid Glamorgan County Council did agree that the Poly should retain the campus at Barry so expansion plans might go ahead. It had been anticipated that having the Barry campus would allow the Poly to expand

Above: Cartoon featured in the South Wales Echo by Gren in 1975

Right: Cartoon from the Students' Union Handbook

to around 4,000 students and it was felt that, without it, the Treforest campus could only cope with up to 3,500 students.

However, leadership for the next phase was passed to a new Director as Dr. James surprised education officials by resigning his post in January 1978 in order to head up a major national research association. Dr. John Davies, a former student of the School of Mines, arrived in September 1978 to work with his Board of Governors on plans to establish a social sciences faculty at Barry – which had quickly looked under-used once it had no new intake of student teachers. But the student body was 'informed' rather than 'consulted' on this plan, and they were having none of it. Students threatened strikes and sit-ins to block the move of around 700 students to Barry which, they said, would *'…change the character of the Polytechnic and…be detrimental to student welfare'.* Given that the majority of the Poly's women students would be in this planned faculty one can understand the 'welfare' issue in question! But they could have saved their energies as the local authority, under further government pressure for financial constraint, made another dramatic volte face. In spite of the Poly's carefully crafted plans for the future of the place, in January 1980 the Mid Glamorgan Education Committee decided that *"The Barry site be withdrawn from use from the Polytechnic of Wales".*

Top: A view of Barry College about 1975

Above: Dr John Davies, Director of the Polytechnic from 1978

Right: Some of the facilities at Barry College

That was it then, one of the shortest mergers in education history and back to a single campus. It's a mercy that not all mergers are so traumatic and short-lived.

Clearly the loss of the second campus didn't result in static student numbers: by 1992, just 11 years after the closure of Barry, the newly inaugurated University of Glamorgan had over 11,500 students enrolled on just one campus. Instead, what had appeared to be a body-blow to the future plans of the institution turned into an opportunity for a major strategic re-think. Some building adaptations and purchases, a different approach to the teaching timetable and other measures were the short-term solutions. A new campus at Glyntaff opened in 1995, and the Atrium in Cardiff opened in November 2007. The lesson from the troubled decade of the Seventies is that with hindsight and something of a Pollyanna attitude, there is rarely a setback that can't be turned into a fresh opportunity.

There is a neat and pleasing circular postscript to the merger and de-merger story of the 1970s. The Glamorganshire Teacher Training College at Barry opened in 1914 for women students as the 'partner' college to the Monmouthshire Teacher Training College at Caerleon for men, which opened in 1913. The similarity of the institutions can be seen in the architecture of the buildings. Caerleon went on to merge with the Newport College of Art and Design and the Gwent College of Technology to form the University of Wales, Newport. The 2013 merger of the University of Glamorgan and the University of Wales, Newport which establishes the University of South Wales therefore largely 'repairs' the unhappy de-merger of the Seventies.

Library

Students' Common Room

CHAPTER 5
Who we are and where we're going:

guessing the story of the University of South Wales

The *University of Glamorgan* is the seventh identity of this institution. Some of the changes in identity have hardly made a ripple in the daily flow of work and they have simply reflected a modest change in circumstances such as a broader curriculum. This was the kind of name change that happened in the early years of World War II when it became the School of Mines and Technology, reflecting that its provision was no longer bound to just the mining industry. As the next century of its existence starts, historically speaking, on the 8th October 2013, it will have assumed its eighth identity: the University of South Wales. This is most likely the single biggest change in operation the institution has faced since it left the management of the Coal Owners and became a local authority owned and managed place. So the overlapping communities of staff, alumni and students have a lot to look back upon, and a lot of assumptions and expectations about the years to come. This part of the centenary book belongs to representative members of the current community; hear their voices through their conversations with Denize McIntyre.

Treforest Campus

Every community has families, and the University's overlapping communities are just the same, with a number of both staff and students that have long standing, intergenerational links with the institution. An example of this is the Deakin – Thomas family.

Q John, as the senior member of your family group, what's the first connection with the University?

"Well, I studied Telecommunications Engineering as a part-time student between 1957 and 1959 – it was a long time ago, the place was a bit different then! I didn't have any idea, of course, that when I started that it was just the beginning, the start, of this link – between us we go on through three generations and it's, well, a span over 50 years! I was pleased when Paula came to study at the Poly".

Q Paula, studied back in the Poly days – what was that like?

"I did my BSc Computer Studies, starting in 1981 and I graduated in 1985.

We were both here at the same time, Malcolm and I. Not on the same course, but this is where we met and later got married, of course. And, now, here we are both teaching at the University: I'm in the Faculty of Advanced Technology and Malcolm is in Health, Sport and Science".

Q How did you meet, exactly?

"Well, we weren't on the same course, but we lived in the same student house in Treforest – I think it's River Street. In fact, there was 18 of us in the house, we all socialised together".

Q That's a lot of students in one house! What was that like?

"It wasn't so good! But there wasn't a lot of accommodation about – it was a big place, it's still there, it had just one bathroom and an outside toilet. Although it was common enough at the time ... for student accommodation to be in a 'distressed state' but, even then there never seemed to be enough of it. I think the landlord had even been struck off the Poly list of 'approved' landlords! He

Right: Three generations of the Deakin-Thomas family explore some of the University's archive documents

162

Deakin-Thomas Family

Former students, current staff members, and current student

used to call around and collect the rent in a Rolls Royce and he was said to have student houses all around the area!"

"Accommodation could be difficult sometimes because the 1980s was a time of major expansion in the student numbers, although the Poly didn't feel like that, as it was very campus-based and had a community feel. No-one ever went off elsewhere, Cardiff for example, to socialise, everything was here and the Otley (or 'O' Block as it became called) was as far as we went".

Q **Ben, tell me about your connections with the University.**

"I'm Ben Thomas, the son of Paula and Malcolm, and John's grandson, so I'm the current student in this line. I'm studying BSc Aeronautical Engineering at Glamorgan, been here since 2009 and, all being well, I'll graduate this summer, 2013. I live locally, too, on Llantwit Road, here in Treforest. But my current student house is normal in having two bathrooms between five students! The house even has two freezers to accommodate the food of just the five of us lads (I'm a member of the University's hockey team, and four of the other hockey lads live in the house)".

Q **What are your strongest memories of your time as students? Or, Ben, What do you think will be your favourite memories?**

Ben: "My hockey matches!"

John: "I particularly recall arriving to discuss the course with some of the lecturers, C.C. Evans and Ivor Dodd. My mate and I came by car, pulled up along the road and asked someone "Where's Treforest Tech?", "Never heard of it" was the reply but that was followed with "but go and try the School of Mines, they'll know!" I also remember travelling to and from home in Caldicot by train and one day in winter 1958 the train pulled into Cardiff – it had snowed a lot – and the newspaper placards were announcing the news of the Manchester United football team being involved in the Munich air crash. And I remember sitting an evening exam which didn't finish until 9.30 p.m. But then I had to take a train to Severn Tunnel Junction, arriving about midnight, but then I had to walk back along the ash path, alongside the track, for two miles to Caldicot – I couldn't see my hand in front of my face as the night was so black!"

Paula: "My memories are around the students' 'Maths and Computing Society', known as the 'Dirty Macs' which had a very strong group identity. I'll always remember the 'interesting' student accommodation and the day the environmental inspection people came around which resulted in the landlord being required to add a second toilet in the building. His solution was to install a toilet in the corner of one lad's room. Only some of the lads would go in there to use it but the lad in question was chuffed, he had his own loo!"

Q **How do you feel about the current period of change, as we mark the 100th birthday? What do you think will change over the next 100 years?**

John: "It's 50 years since I was here and you couldn't have had the first idea that it would become what it has, expand like this. It was just the School of Mines. Although it had changed names people still called it that!"

Ben: "It will be hard to think of the other two Gwent campuses as being a part of the Uni, though the Glyntaff campus feels like a part, it seems less so for the Atrium, but I think

this will pass. It'll happen that strong communities will be built on the five sites, students will identify, for example, with the University of South Wales at Caerleon, or the University of South Wales at Treforest, or wherever".

Paula: "I'm anticipating travelling to Newport to teach on one day a week in the future".

Ben: "Some of the subjects offered by the University now will still be around for future generations, I think ...but just keep advancing, maybe it will be space travel or space engineering".

Paula: "The way we teach changes, rather than the subjects. Distance learning could develop but it depends on the subject. Some subjects need the student to do something in a lab, be practical – for example, Dad studied

telecommunications engineering, and it's still there, just a 2013 version".

Ben agreed: "It might be that virtual environments will develop to such an extent that some learning can be done in a classroom which is currently much more difficult – students may be able to walk around a virtual rainforest."

Q **What might you want to say to students of the future?**

Ben: "Work hard, play hard. Do all your work, do your coursework, but then enjoy yourself and get the balance right".

John: "The basics have been set for years, but it's for you to improve on it the best you can".

Paula: "It doesn't matter whether you study part-time or full time, just progress."

Anna Leidig

Student: Science Foundation Year

In March 2013, Anna is the University's youngest student. She is 17 years old, and will be 18 on 14th March. Anna's home is in Kilkenny in the Republic of Ireland but she is half German, and is fluent in the language. She has two brothers, one at Swansea University and the other still at school. Anna thinks Glamorgan is attractive to students from Ireland as the travelling is easier either by ferry or by air and it's less difficult than, for example, going to college in Galway. Anna had previously been to boarding school in Dublin, so moving away from home wasn't a new thing.

Q Why did you choose Glamorgan?

"Well, I didn't actually choose Glamorgan as my first choice University – I made a late choice in clearing. The course is a one-year Science Foundation which covers a broad range of science modules including some I like more than others! But it's good because after completing it I'll be able to choose from a range of degree courses. I'm using it to apply for Pharmaceutical Sciences around the UK".

Q So what's your average week like, what occupies your time?

"My working week at University means Friday is free all day and so are alternate Thursdays, but these clear days means Monday has a packed timetable: from 11.00 a.m. to 7.00 p.m. Tuesday is about the same but I think it's manageable as there's a 2 hour gap in which it's possible to get a meal. I also have a part-time job – I work 6 hours a week as a support worker for another student who has Asperger's syndrome. I like it – I take care of him including getting him out and about to socialise, we go shopping, into the park etc and the aim is that it helps improve his social skills. I've also worked part-time in the Students' Union on the reception desk!"

Q What do you think is the best part of studying at Glamorgan?

"My favourite thing is the sports facilities! I play hockey and there are sports facilities here that other universities just don't have. After I've left the place, say years ahead, I think it'll probably be the social life around my sport that I'll remember most. Although I'll also remember the fun (and challenges!) of living in our student house on Llantwit Road with four rugby playing lads! The social life with the hockey team is great fun. After our matches, the girls like to go out dressed up following a theme. Most recently, after the last match of the spring term, our theme was Television – so I went as a Smurf complete with blue skin! Some of our other themes have been 'the Army' and 'Onesies' (a type of pyjama in one piece)."

Q How has the merger of Glamorgan and Newport affected you as a student?

"Well, I've heard about it but it hasn't touched our student group very much at this stage and so I don't yet have a feel for what the student experience will be like."

Q Thinking further ahead, say a generation away, what's your prediction for what learning will be like at a University?

"There's definitely not going to be any books! I don't think so anyway, everything will be on tablets, including notes for classes and textbooks, all of it. Neither will students in the future write anything down. And it might be the case that practical experiences, more

application of science, will be put into courses meaning they become more 'hands-on'. In pharmaceutical sciences (what I want to do next) I think changes are likely to be dramatic and maybe involve new ways of delivering drugs, for instance. And I'm not sure that future universities will need classrooms as I think perhaps there won't be any lectures, but learning may all take place on-line. Wouldn't it be sad, though, if students didn't go away to University? There's other, wider experiences like meeting new people. It just wasn't an option for me to stay at home as there wasn't a nearby university, but I'm glad it pushed me into the experience."

Q What might you want to say to students of the future?

"My message to students years away from now would be about what I learned about feeling homesick. I'm sure that if I hadn't joined the hockey team there was probably a 90% chance that I would have dropped out of University and gone back home because I was very homesick. I made friends on my course, but I think students are better off with a big circle of friends. So I'd tell new students to join plenty of societies as it will keep you busy and make sure you always have something to do or somewhere to go. So you fill your time and keep your mind off homesickness. Doing these other things, possibly with part-time work, is an important part of your student experience."

University of
South Wales
Prifysgol
De Cymru

Library Services

Norman Morris

Norman Morris is, in the spring term of 2013, the University of Glamorgan's longest serving employee, and on the 8th July 2013 he will have completed 50 years service. He was born in Porth, Rhondda, where he still lives. Norman is based on the Glyntaff campus in the beautiful listed building which was originally a girls' grammar school. In Norman's time the institution has had four identities: The Glamorgan College of Technology, Glamorgan Polytechnic, The Polytechnic of Wales, and the University of Glamorgan. He will also see in the University of South Wales.

Q Norman, tell us about your earliest connection with the College.

"I had a loose association with the college from a young age. Once a year on a Sunday, many valleys people would move en mass down to the seaside for the church or chapel outing. We travelled on the train to Barry and the line ran above the then small college campus, and that railway line is now the Treforest campus central car park!"

"Later, when I was studying for a pre-apprenticeship qualification I started applying for jobs and the first offer I had came from the (then) Glamorgan College of Technology, and I accepted it. I was 15 when I arrived and I worked for two years as a junior laboratory technician in the Mining Department under the care of a senior technician, a proper old character, Mervyn Jones, who was more affectionately known as 'Jones the Coal'."

Q Do you remember much about your first day?

"I clearly remember that day and that early period – parts of Brecon Building were new, and it had Electrical and Mechanical Engineering laboratories along the ground floor and Geology and

Staff Member: Higher Technical Officer, Faculty of Health, Sport and Science

Mining laboratories upstairs where the Finance office is now. I also worked in the 'Two foot nine', which was our name for the mine roadway which had been built by mining industry apprentices and is still underneath the Brecon Building arts workshop. The campus was really different then, it more or less ended behind Brecon, although there were some tin huts where Dyffryn Block is now; the rest of the campus was just fields, there was no central roadway."

Q 50 years is such an achievement, how does that feel?

"I have mixed feelings about it being 50 years – when I think about it I can't believe where the years have gone, but I also know how fortunate I've been to have this stability and to be working at the time the retirement legislation changed to give me the chance to stay longer."

Q Your time covers many changes – what's the most significant?

"The biggest change I recall was when the college changed from the 'College of Technology' to 'Glamorgan Polytechnic'. Other changes, such as changing from a Poly to a University didn't feel like a major change. Courses have changed – the old National Certificate and Higher National Certificates have been phased out, or passed to partner colleges to run. But the University still feels much the same to me as it did, I have affection for the place and my daughter graduated from here, and my son

Above: Norman Morris as a teenager – shortly before joining the staff

169

did a Higher Technical Certificate in Mechanical Engineering – Glamorgan feels a lucky place."

"In my faculty, technicians' jobs have changed a lot, mostly as a result of more sophisticated machines and specialised equipment. Some technicians are also now called 'Technical Demonstrators' which reflects that the courses make use of their skills and in-depth knowledge of the machines."

Q In what ways do you think students have changed?

"Students are much the same as they were, I think. There's the same range of personalities and characters as there was. I remember more about research students as I spend more time in the lab with them. There was a chap who was a chieftain's son, he always wore a smart white suit and had all the perfumes – he was a larger than life character. Then a tall African student called Jonathan who was as easily heard as seen as he had a big, booming voice. And more recently, there's Alessandro, or Alex, who worked for a battery company in Ebbw Vale on the old steelworks site – he was such an enthusiastic person, which is very infectious".

Q With your experiences, what do you predict for the future of the Uni?

"Thinking about the future, I think the Uni might continue with expansion, drawing in more colleges. I think a core of subjects might stay the same but there'll be new courses added and that information technology will have an even greater place in how students learn as I can see how my

Below: Norman at work with modern laboratory equipment

three year-old grand-daughter uses a tablet computer even for playing and colouring pictures. I hope all learning isn't done through computers, though, as I think that might take something away from the experience of learning. I've wondered how new subjects will emerge and it's hard to tell, but something will spring from someone's imagination and off it will go! It could be something that we dismiss right now but which will be developed into a major subject. And there's always rocks! Perhaps interplanetary geology! But I think that the majority of future students will want the bigger experiences that coming to university can offer so we'll still need campuses as now. I'd like to think that some of our best buildings will still be around in another hundred years – Ty Crawshay (A Block) is looking really good and well cared for, and it will be interesting to see if other, newer buildings on the campus last as long."

Q What might you want to say to students of the future?

"I'd like to tell the next generation of students and staff in the future University that education is an essential investment for a better future and will always be necessary. Lifelong learning begins at birth and stays with you for the rest of your life. It's no different; it will always be like that."

Above: Norman (back row, far left) at a science summer school in the 1970s

David Lewis

David Jonathan Arwel Lewis is 43 years old and a self-labelled 'local boy from Merthyr Tydfil'. He is the Manager of the Blended Learning, Media Services and Desktop Development teams. This covers support for learning systems (Blackboard or Questionmark), the development of online degrees, and the introduction of innovations such as Module Evaluation and the Panopto Lecture Capture System. These things link to other responsibilities for Media Services, which looks after the classroom development and deployment of audio-visual and media. Underpinning this is a team which manages the services to desktop users, such as operating system and applications, printing, or anti-virus updating.

Q Was your first connection with the Uni when you were appointed to this job?

"No! Like many staff and students, I've got long-standing connections with the University. When I was a boy I was particularly impressed by a work colleague of my father's who was doing a Masters course in Computing and this, to me, was "Wow – a Rocket Scientist!" My grandfather, my father-in-law, other family members and a number of my friends are all former students of the University. And, really, as a child I couldn't travel by train up or down the valley without looking across at the University and longing to be inside where the computers were! Then, after graduating, I was lucky and moved into a career which met my passion for applying computing to enhance processes – in this case, it's learning!"

Staff member: Blended Learning Manager

Q **So, what is your job entailing right now in 2013?**

"Well, the team is doing a lot of thinking about the University's merger with the University of Wales, Newport, but we're also working on a number of projects which you could say are at the cutting edge of learning technology. For example, we are in the process of updating Blackboard (our virtual learning environment) with new and exciting features that couldn't have been thought of just 10 years ago – like the ability to find Facebook friends through Blackboard, or manage classroom activity through Facebook. The team is looking forward to being able to remotely connect to a computer at, for example, the Newport city campus and resolve their classroom IT problem quicker than we can currently walk across the Treforest campus to a classroom from our base in Johnstown Building."

Q **It's been said that there's a 'feel' about Glamorgan – what do you think?**

"Yes, Glamorgan has a very, very strong sense of community. And it's embedded in this geographic community. We are both part of the community and we have our own graduate community."

Q **How do you think students' experiences might change at the bigger, merged university?**

"They'll identify with their course or their own location, as most do now. Students at the Atrium currently identify with their Cardiff location and nursing students currently identify with Glyntaff more than Treforest. Having five campuses will mean that this identity is stronger locally and even activities might consolidate locally. In the long term, perhaps 30 or 40 years time, even with more technological advances, the merged university will still have five campuses as academics say that even for a smaller number of undergraduates the current physical space we have doesn't accommodate modern teaching methods. Advances such as simulation suites for nursing or hands-on learning for aero engineering... these are very space 'needy', but this type of teaching currently has to be done in specific way to get the valuable professional accreditation students want. There could be some technological solutions to some of this – such as having one multipurpose room which can be adapted. An example exists at an English university which has a massive 250 seat lecture theatre which, at the touch of a button, can transform into a space for a different purpose. But that button takes 20 minutes to do the transformation – so there are timetabling issues around that change-over."

Q Can the University cope with big technological changes like that?

"Yes! Glamorgan is in a position to adapt quickly to new innovations but, really, it's not the matter which changes but the process for learning. Whereas our original engineers sat in lines with blackboard and chalk, now it's a personal computer with PowerPoint and projector, but we are working on new technology called 'Panopto' which is a system for capturing a lecture and broadcasting it. This would mean that if we had a fantastic Marketing lecturer who happened to work from the Newport campus then Caerleon or Treforest could take part in the same lecture, with students interacting. Although I think students would still come to a campus, rather than watch this lecture at home, because learning is a social activity: both the knowledge and the interaction are important – it's a human need. I know that students studying entirely on-line come together to discuss the differences in perspectives, exchange views...it's a human need."

Q So what other challenges do you imagine are still to come?

"We know now that students are studying on degrees but many of them will be employed in a job which doesn't yet exist! That's how quick the environment changes these days. But if you compared many University subjects from 40 years ago to what's studied now, then much is the same but how knowledge is used will change. For example, manufacturing is going to be turned on its head by 3D printing, business will be turned upside down by a massive global market with linkages anywhere on the globe: somebody could be working in a shed in Carmarthen but providing a vital link to a process in Timbuktu. The University must turn out graduates who are able to work with people they will never see and cross-boundary communication will be a key skill."

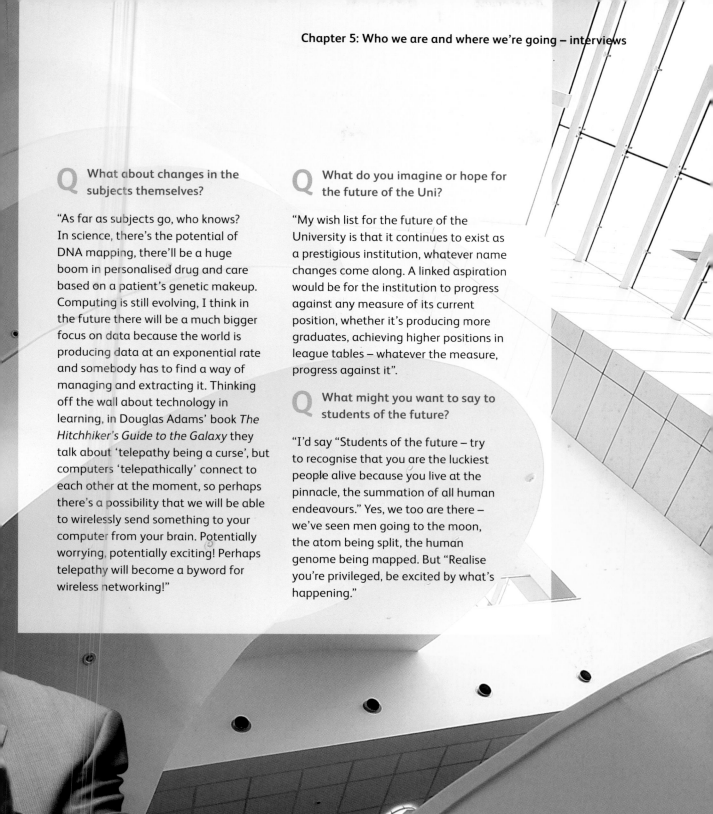

Q What about changes in the subjects themselves?

"As far as subjects go, who knows? In science, there's the potential of DNA mapping, there'll be a huge boom in personalised drug and care based on a patient's genetic makeup. Computing is still evolving, I think in the future there will be a much bigger focus on data because the world is producing data at an exponential rate and somebody has to find a way of managing and extracting it. Thinking off the wall about technology in learning, in Douglas Adams' book *The Hitchhiker's Guide to the Galaxy* they talk about 'telepathy being a curse', but computers 'telepathically' connect to each other at the moment, so perhaps there's a possibility that we will be able to wirelessly send something to your computer from your brain. Potentially worrying, potentially exciting! Perhaps telepathy will become a byword for wireless networking!"

Q What do you imagine or hope for the future of the Uni?

"My wish list for the future of the University is that it continues to exist as a prestigious institution, whatever name changes come along. A linked aspiration would be for the institution to progress against any measure of its current position, whether it's producing more graduates, achieving higher positions in league tables – whatever the measure, progress against it".

Q What might you want to say to students of the future?

"I'd say "Students of the future – try to recognise that you are the luckiest people alive because you live at the pinnacle, the summation of all human endeavours." Yes, we too are there – we've seen men going to the moon, the atom being split, the human genome being mapped. But "Realise you're privileged, be excited by what's happening."

Atrium, Cardiff

Hannah Sanderson and Joshua Spence

Students: traditional Mathematics and new Fashion Design

Josh and Hannah between them represent 100 years of subjects taught at Glamorgan, and how those subjects reflect the industries and services of their time. Maths was there in the original curriculum for the mining engineers. Fashion Design is among the newest subjects offered and it's taught on the newest campus, at the Atrium in Cardiff.

Q Hannah, can you tell us something about yourself?

"I'm a final year student, in my fourth year, as I spent a placement year working for four months in Finland at a fashion school which specialised in leatherwear and knitwear. Then I followed that by placements in London working for top designer Kanye West and up-and-coming designer Jonathan Saunders. I didn't have any connection, family etc, with the Uni before I came here to study."

Q Josh – what are you doing?

"I'm currently on the first year of the BSc Mathematics course, but I studied the foundation year for maths in academic year 2011-12. Me neither – no connections with the Uni before arriving here."

Q How did both of you find settling in here?

Hannah: "I'd been at a sixth form college in Devon and, before that, at a private school in Buckinghamshire but when I arrived here at Glamorgan I felt I'd found my place, this is where I belong. I've met people with the same interests, and kind of at the same level as me."

Josh: "Before Uni I took four years out. I worked for a couple of years, then travelled for two and half years to Canada, USA, Europe, New Zealand, Australia and Hong Kong – Yep, a very lucky man. When I came back, there were options for a job, but not very well paid. I considered Glamorgan or a college in London, so I made the decision because of the rankings in the University League Table produced by newspapers – Glamorgan was one of the best in the UK for Maths. My parents and sister all have a background in maths or engineering, so I never thought about much else, no rebellion!"

Q **What do you both think about the other's subjects – they're really different?**

Josh: "I think my course reflects my personal approach to stuff – I'm a very logical thinker. I approach Maths in a step-by-step way and I can problem-solve. Maths requires you to do this, but I couldn't start with a blank bit of paper in the way that creative people, designers do! Though maybe mathematicians can be creative in a particular way, I mean in maths you have to be creative to think outside the box to see a way around a problem, and I can do that. For example, in some maths problems you have to split it up to be able to solve it. If you go down the wrong route then you can take 10 times longer to solve it. Spot what to do, be creative to move numbers around."

Hannah: "Yes – creativity, but different! With my course, Fashion Design, it's more like do anything you want to do! Go bonkers! Take your blank paper and open your mind! I don't know whether that sort of open-mindedness is natural or if it could be taught, in the way that Maths can probably be taught. I think the biggest differences in these subjects of ours are around subjectivity – mine is a very subjective subject and Josh's is the opposite."

Q **So you DO think each other is doing a 'proper' subject?**

Josh: "Yes! Respect! It's essential to have a natural creativity for art or design. People think Maths is difficult. Then I get pigeon-holed. Because they might struggle with maths they think I must be so clever!"

Hannah: "Yes again! At school I absolutely couldn't do maths so my parents spent a lot of money on tutors but they had no success to show for it! So I have that same reaction – I'm impressed and jealous that Josh can do that! People's reaction to my subject is around it being a 'proper' subject. "You just draw all day" I get told. I answer "Yes, I draw, but for a reason – I clothe you! It's so important…""

Atrium, Cardiff

Q **What about the reputation of your subjects from Glamorgan?**

Josh: "It'll have a strong future, and there'll be other ways of applying it. There's financial maths, statistics, engineering maths, and there's a newish subject 'Computing Maths' which I think will become a lot bigger. The Maths at Glam is so good, and so is the research – some here is world class. In Germany and China they carry good reputations for maths but a high percentage of Glamorgan's research is internationally recognised and some is world leading. It's good to be a part of this."

Hannah: "I feel that, as fashion is a newer subject at the University (all Uni's, really) it's still building a strong reputation. Fashion design is currently a very London-centric business, but this course will be more established soon and be in the position that maths is in now. I also feel it's much more important for me to build my own reputation as a fashion designer and then I'll be contributing to Glamorgan's reputation!"

Q **What are your predictions for what learning will be like when the Uni celebrates its 200th anniversary?**

Hannah: "They might have floating screens that can be where the students are!"

Josh: "It'll be like science fiction.... electronics will have a massive impact.

Like, if they don't go to Uni then they can still see all the lectures – But no way is that a good idea!"

Hannah: "Absolutely agree! For my degree not attending would be horrendous. I can see a place for continuing with low technology – I do most illustration using a software package such as Photoshop, but I still have to have my sketch pad and just draw – it's just nice to be able to push ideas onto paper. Creative industries will be massive in the future, it's massive now, but I think the issue of sensible payment for internships needs sorting out. Students can't work for long hours and be unpaid."

Q **What might you want to say to students of the future?**

Josh: "Enjoy uni! Learn as much as you can and enjoy everything as much as you can. Meet and enjoy people. You've got another 30 or 40 years of working, so make the most of this time. Get up earlier to make the most of it! And if you're studying here in Cardiff or Pontypridd then buy an umbrella!!!!"

Hannah: "Students – you should manage your time well, pace yourself and don't leave things to the last minute...simply enjoy it. The rain will be the same, but maybe they'll have invented a digital umbrella that follows you about! You'll need a designer and a mathematician together for that! Ha ha!"

Professor Knox's last word

Written in October 1928

It seems completely proper to leave the last words in this commemorative book to the man who set the standards and the ethos from day one: Professor George Knox. In a report entitled *The South Wales and Monmouthshire School of Mines, Treforest & Crumlin: Report Upon the Work of Session 1927-28* (the final year the School was managed by the Coal Owners' Association), Professor Knox includes a note of appreciation and says:

"Whatever the future of the School may be, its founders, and those who have been associated with them in carrying out the work, can always look back with pleasure on the results achieved. The School has reached a recognised high standard of educational attainment and its students are to be found in almost every civilised country and from the reports received they are, without exception, doing credit to themselves and to the School."

As we, the current community of staff and students, stand at the end of the first century, and face a new century with a new identity, we can feel quietly confident that they would be proud. The founders, Professor Knox and the earliest of our students, would recognise the place today. The community feel is the same, the pride in achievement is the same, and the links with industry are the same. These are the characteristics which made the School of Mines, and we have managed to hang onto these values through management change, world wars and recessions.

The University of South Wales could not set a more apt goal for the institution in the coming century: more of the same, please.

Proff. Knox

The passing of Professor GEORGE KNOX, the first Principal of the School of Mines, in November last, at the age of 81, was felt as a personal loss by all associated with the School, and particularly by the older generation of students.

Born in Ayrshire n 1869, he commenced his mining career with the Dalmellington Iron Company, and obtained his Colliery Managers' Certificate at the age of 23. In 1894 he accepted a post as Lecturer in Mining under the Ayrshire County Council, and his success in organising the first Course System of Evening Classes in Mining Engineering was recognised in 1904, when he was appointed Head of the Mining Department at the Wigan Mining and Technical College.

When a group of the South Wales Coal Owners decided, in 1912, to establish, and finance, an institution to provide advanced technological instruction, for the training of all grades of officials engaged in and about the mines, he was entrusted with the task of organisation under the title of "Director of Mining Studies."

Within six months of the date of his appointment—Forest House, Treforest, was purchased, equipped and staffed, to serve as a Central School for the Coalfield under the title of the South Wales and Monmouthshire School of Mines. It was opened in October, 1193, to provide facilities for full time Courses in Mining, Surveying, Mechanical and Electrical Engineering and Chemistry, and for part-time Day Courses for students released from industry on one day per week. The School at Crumlin to serve as a centre for part-time day courses for the Monmouthshire area was opened a year later.

The Scheme of Study introduced was widely recognised as providing unique features, and the Government of India eventually established, at Dhanbad, an institution on the same lines as Treforest.

In the course of years, the Schools of Mines at Treforest and Crumlin became such an integral part of the Technical Education of Glamorgan and Monmouthshire that it was considered desirable, in 1928, by the Mining Industrialists to transfer the administration and financing of the Schools to the Local Education Authorities.

A man of wide interests, Principal Knox rendered valuable service in many fields. He gave evidence on Mining matters before several Government Commissions, and represented technical teachers on the Burnham Technical Committee.

An expert Geoglist, his paper on "Landslides and Mining Subsidence in South Wales" received widespread recognition, and he was awarded the Gold Medal of the South Wales Institute of Engineers. Elected President in 1929, his outstanding services were further recognised by election to Honorary Membership in 1940.

He was a keen Golfer, a popular member and past Captain of Radyr Golf Club.

Principal Knox retired in 1931, and some years later returned to Scotland with Mrs. Knox, whom he has predeceased, to spend the evening of their days in their native Ayrshire.

Professor Knox's obituary from the students' magazine, Breccia, 1951

On equal terms

> **1913-1931**

Prof George Knox

1935-1940

Mr Robert James
(Acting Principal 1931-35)

1940-1949

South Wales and Monmouthshire School of Mines

School of Mines and Technology

1970-1973

1973-1975

Dr D.W Francis James

1975-1978

Glamorgan Polytechnic

Polytechnic of Wales

Principals

1949-1952	1952-1958	1958–1970
	Dr David P. Evans	
Glamorgan Technical College		Glamorgan College of Technology

1978-1992	1993-2005	2005-2010	>
Dr John D. Davies	Prof Sir Adrian Webb	Prof David Halton	
	University of Glamorgan		

1913-2010

> **2010-2013**
>
> Prof Julie Lydon

2013-

Prof Julie Lydon

University of Glamorgan

University of South Wales

Principals

184

Business School

2010-2013

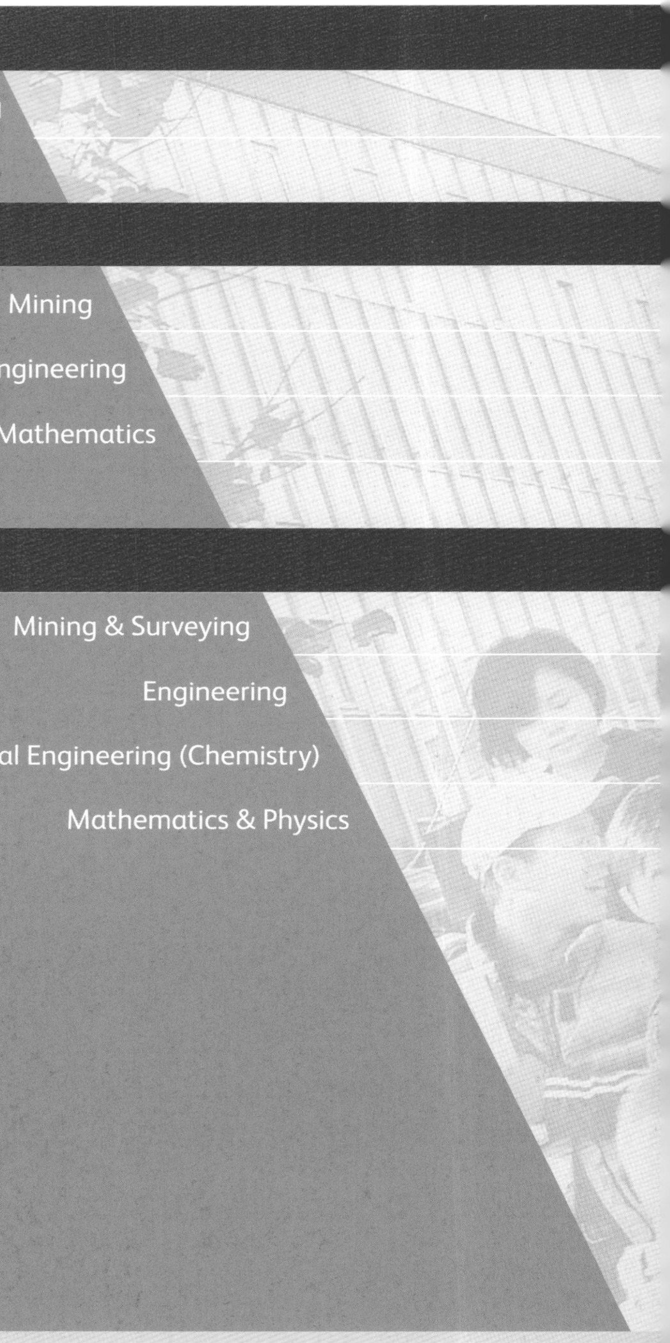

1913

Mining

1932

Mining

Electrical Engineering

Mechanical Engineering & Mathematics

1947

Mining & Surveying

Engineering

Fuel Technology & Chemical Engineering (Chemistry)

Mathematics & Physics

Department

Growth of departments

South Wales and Monmouthshire School of Mines

Professor George Knox, F.G.S., M.I.M.E.

South Wales and Monmouthshire School of Mines

Richard Richards, M.I.Min.E, M.I.M.S.

William Winterbottom Firth, M.Sc, A.R.C.S

Robert James, Wh.Sch., A.R.C.S., D.I.C., A.M.I.Mech.E.

School of Mines and Technology

Thomas Powell, M.Sc., M.I.Min.E, M.I.M.S

John Jordan, M.Sc., Ph.D.

John A. Benjamin, B.Sc., A.R.I.C.

C. Cyril Evans, M.Sc.

Department Heads

1913-1947

1963

Mechanical & Production Engineering

Civil Engineering & Building

Electrical Engineering

Mining & Mining Surveying

Chemistry & Chemical Engineering

Physics & Mathematics

Commerce & Administration

1970

Business Studies

Chemical Engineering

Chemistry

Civil Engineering & Building

Electrical Engineering

Management Studies

Mathematics & Computer Science

Mechanical & Production Engineering

Mining & Mine Surveying

Physics

Department

Growth of departments

Glamorgan College of Technology

John Jordan, M.Sc., Ph.D.

Ron D. McMurray, B.Sc., A.M.I.C.E.

David M. Dummer, A.M.I.E.E, A.M.I.Mech.E.

Herbert P. Richards, B.Sc., M.I.Min.E., Dip.Met.Min.

Leo H. Thomas, M.Sc., F.R.I.C.

C. Cyril Evans, M.Sc., F.Inst.P., A.M.Brit.I.R.E

Ken Oglethorpe, B.Com., A.M.B.I.M

Glamorgan Polytechnic

Ken Oglethorpe, B.Com., A.M.B.I.M

Gwilym Bolan, B.Sc., C.Eng., M.I.Chem.E., M.Inst.F.

Leo H. Thomas, M.Sc., F.R.I.C.

Ron D. McMurray, B.Sc., C.Eng., F.I.C.E., F.I.O.B.

David M. Dummer, C.Eng., M.I.E.E, M.I.Mech.E.

Ron Roberts, B.Sc. (Econ.), M.I.P.M., M.B.I.M.

Douglas J. Green, M.Sc., D.I.C., F.B.C.S., F.I.M.A.

Mike B. Bassett, M.Sc (Tech.), Ph.D., C.Eng., M.I.Mech.E., M.I.Prod.E.

Albert J. Gibbon, B.Sc., C.Eng., F.I.Min.E., Dip.Met.Min.

H. J. Shepherd, B.Sc., A.Inst.P.

Department Heads

1963-1970

1977

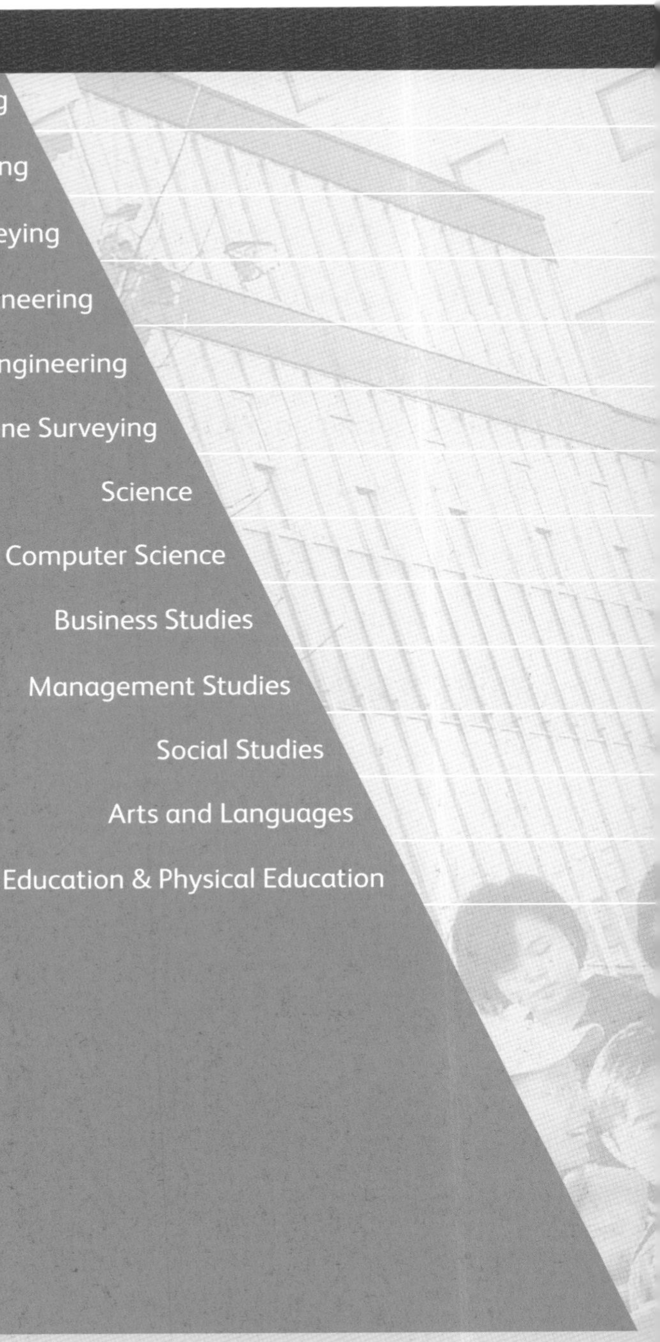

Chemical Engineering

Civil Engineering & Building

Estate Management and Quantity Surveying

Electrical Engineering

Mechanical & Production Engineering

Mining & Mine Surveying

Science

Mathematics & Computer Science

Business Studies

Management Studies

Social Studies

Arts and Languages

Education & Physical Education

Department

Growth of departments

The Polytechnic of Wales

Len Lee (Acting Head of Dept.), B.Sc.,C.Eng., M.Inst.F.

Ron D. McMurray, B.Sc., C.Eng., F.I.C.E., F.I.O.B.

Anthony J. Biker, M.Sc., A.R.I.C.S., A.R.V.A.

David M. Dummer, C.Eng., M.I.E.E, M.I.Mech.E.

Mike B. Bassett, M.Sc. (Tech), Ph.D., C.Eng., F.I.Mech.E., M.I.Prod.E., F.I.Plant.E.

Lewin Morgan, C.Eng., F.R.I.C.S., F.I.Min.E.

William O. George, B.Sc., Ph.D., D.Sc., C.Chem., F.R.I.C.

Graham G. L. Wright, M.A., F.B.C.S.

Gavin Thomas (Acting Head of Dept.), B.Sc., Dip.Ed.

Ron Roberts, M.Sc., B.Sc. (Econ.), M.I.P.M., M.B.I.M.

Peter J. L. Hawkins, B.A., B.Sc. (Soc), M.Sc. (Econ), A.M.B.I.M.

Michael Slater, M.A.

W. R. Lotwick, M.Sc.

Department Heads

1977

2012

Computing & Mathematical Sciences

Electronics & Computer Systems Engineering

Engineering

Environmental Technology, Construction & Management

Animation & Visual Effects

Communication Design & Photography

Drama

Fashion & Retail Design

Media

Music & Sound

Science & Sport

Care Sciences

Professional Education & Service Delivery

Business School

Psychology

Humanities & Social Sciences

Law, Accounting & Finance

Department

Growth of departments

University of Glamorgan (Final department structure)

Andrew Ware, B.Sc., M.Sc., Ph.D., F.B.C.S.

Lee Jones, B.Sc., Ph.D., C.Eng.

Steven Wilcox, B.Sc., Ph.D., C.Eng., F.I.Mech.E.

Dawn Story, B.Sc., Pg.C., Ph.D., C.M.I.O.S.H., F.H.E.A.

Peter Hodges, M.A., B.Ed.

Huw Swayne, B.A., Pg.Dip., F.H.E.A.

Lisa Lewis

Tracy Pritchard

Rob Campbell, B.A., M.A., R.S.A.Cert.

Paul Carr, Ph.D., L.L.C.M., B.A.

Christopher Lee, B.Sc., M.Sc., Ph.D., Pg.C.E.

Ruth Davis, Ph.D., M.Phil., B.N., R.N., N.D.N.Cert., Pg.C.E.

Linda Evans, Ph.D., M.B.A., Dip.H.R.M., B.Ed.

Andrew Rogers, M.Sc., B.Ed., Dip. In Nursing, R.M.N., R.N.T., Ph.D.

Peter Mayer, B.Sc., Ph.D.

Andrew Thompson, B.A., Ph.D.

Donna Whitehead

Department Heads

2012

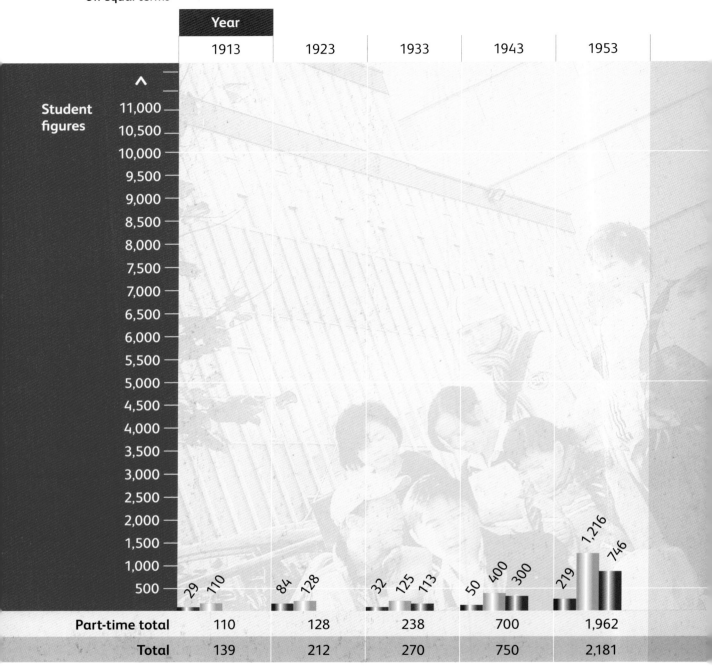

On equal terms

Year	1913	1923	1933	1943	1953
Student figures	29, 110	84, 128	32, 125, 113	50, 400, 300	219, 1,216, 746
Part-time total	110	128	238	700	1,962
Total	139	212	270	750	2,181

Student figures

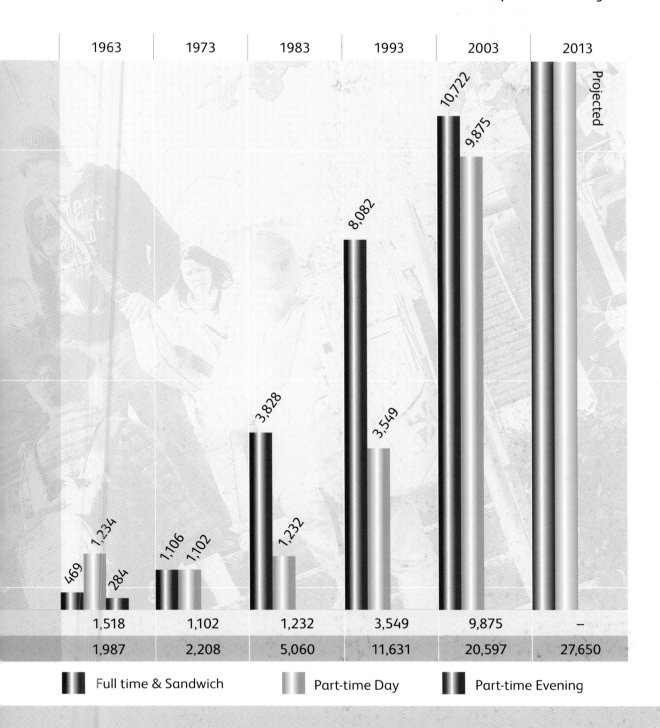

	1963	1973	1983	1993	2003	2013
						Projected
Full time & Sandwich	469	1,106	3,828	8,082	10,722	
	1,234	1,102	1,232	3,549	9,875	
Part-time Evening	284					
Part-time Day	1,518	1,102	1,232	3,549	9,875	–
	1,987	2,208	5,060	11,631	20,597	27,650

■ Full time & Sandwich   ■ Part-time Day   ■ Part-time Evening

1913-2013

Campus	Current buildings
Treforest	Ty Crawshay (A Block)
	Brecon Building (B Block)
	Cynon Building (C Block)
	Duffryn (D Block)
	Ferndale (formerly called Forest Hall)
	Glynneath (G Block)
	Hirwaun (H Block)
	Johnstown (J Block)
	Kidwelly (K Block)
	Learning Resources Centre
	Health Centre (T Block)
	Wenvoe Building (W Block)
	The Meeting House (X Block)
	Students' Union
	Recreation Centre
	Creche
	Refectory/Stilts
	Aerospace Centre
	Glamorgan Conference centre
	Forest Grove houses
	Prospect House, Innovation House, and Academic Registry
	Welsh Institute of Chiropractic
	Research Office

The buildings

Date built, purchased or opened for University	Details
1912	Acquired for the School of Mines
1913	New laboratory wing added ready for opening of the School
1957	Stage 1 – Mining, Electrical Engineering, Physics and telecommunications. (middle section of B block)
1962	Stage 2 – at opening included the departments of Civil Engineering and Building, Chemical Engineering, Commerce and Administration, and additions to Physics and Mathematics
1963	Stage 3 – New administration block, college hall, library, lower refectory, Students' Union Office and Common Room
circa 1963	Originally a teaching block, now Students Services
circa 1972	-
1967	The first student hostel
1972	Built for the department of Civil Engineering and Building
1972/3	Built for departments of Business Studies, Management Studies and Social Studies & Arts
1976	Built for departments of Mathematics, Computer Science and IT Centre
1957	Originally the Production Engineering workshops
1972	Phase 1
1988	Phase 2
circa 1991	-
1972 and 2002	Estates building and stores
circa 1972	Also known as the Chapliancy Centre
1972	First Students' Union
2010	New Students' Union re-biilt on the site of the original
1989	-
1995	An earlier temporary creche was located elsewhere on the campus
1972/3	-
2010	-
1997	-
from 1995 onward	-
from 1995 to 1999	-
2000	-
Late 1930s	Originally built as the Caretaker's House

1912-2013

On equal terms

Johnstown (J Block)

198

Business School

Crawshay's Cafe

Glynneath (G Block)

Glynneath (G Block)

Students' Union

Stilts Food Court

Campus	Current buildings
Lower Glyntaff	Tramsheds
	Elaine Morgan Building
	Welsh Institute for Health and Social Care
	Aneurin Bevan Building
Upper Glyntaff	Professor Bernard Knight Building
	Alfred Russell Wallace Building
	George Knox Building

Detail fom George Knox Building, Upper Glyntaff Campus

The buildings

Date built, purchased or opened for University	Details
circa 2003-4	-
1995	-
1995	-
2005	-
	-
2009	-
2009	Originally built as a girls' grammar school
2009	-

Alfred Russell Wallace Building, Upper Glyntaff Campus

1912-2013

Campus	Current building
Cardiff	The Atrium

Atrium, Cardiff

The buildings

Date built, purchased or opened for University	Details
2007	-

1912-2013

Guess
the honoraries

1. Mr Benjamin Zephaniah, DLitt 2011; 2. Lord Michael Heseltine, DUniv 2013; 3. Mr Neil Jenkins MBE, Chancellor's Medal 2000; 4. Mr Grenfell Jones MBE, DUniv 1999; 5. Mr Gerald Davies, DUniv 1999; 6. Ms Jo Brand, DUniv 2007; 7. Mr Griff Rhys Jones, DLitt 2005; 8. Mr Mark Hughes MBE, Chancellor's Medal 2003; 9. Baroness Grey-Thompson DBE, Chancellor's Medal 2001; 10. Mr Huw Stephens, Honorary Fellowship 2012; 11. Dr Rowan Williams, DUniv 2013; 12. Mr Huw Edwards, DUniv 2007; 13. Lord Richard Attenborough, DUniv 2005; 14. Mr Colin Jackson CBE, Chancellor's Medal 2005.

More honoraries: Dr Gwyn Jones, Honorary Fellowship 1991; Mr Simon Weston OBE, DUniv 1994; Mr J P R Williams MBE, DUniv 1996; Mr Max Boyce MBE, Chancellor's Medal 2000; Sir Patrick Moore, DSc 2001; Mr Dennis O'Neill CBE, LLD 2003; Mr Roy Noble OBE DL OSt J, Chancellor's Medal 2009; Mr Scott Quinnell, Chancellor's Medal 2009; Ms Shami Chakrabarti CBE, DUniv 2011.

Acknowledgements

I am grateful for all the help I have received during the writing of this book, and for permissions to use images old and new. As the help was limitless but my memory is not, if I have inadvertently been forgetful, please be assured that I am really grateful.

From the University: Julie Lydon, Vice Chancellor, for commissioning and supporting the production of the book; Dr Christopher Lee, for additional insight into the Mining and Geology courses; Professor Hugh Coombs, Professor of Accounting, for advice on the historic structures of local government; Dr Gareth Jones, Clive Bennett and Daren Crocker, for stories and information relating to the dinosaur; Kath Gould, Senior Graphic Designer, for infinite patience and assistance with scanning images and documents and her colleague, Claire Evans, for further scanning of images; Ceri Carter, Research Assistant, for her willing and tenacious work; Daniel Porter-Jones, for professional support and encouragement; Dr Ceri Thomas, for providing his father's biographic detail and photographs; the late Basil Isaac, without whose interest in the early history of the School of Mines, much information may have been lost; Alan Holloway and Rosemary Bailey, for compiling Alan's personal memories, and permission to use photographs; the following students and colleagues for generously agreeing to be interviewed and photographed, or providing personal photographs: Norman Morris, Senior Technical Officer; Ben Thomas, final year student; Paula Thomas, Subject Leader for Information Technology and former student; John Deakin, former student; Anna Leidig, current student; Josh Spence, current student; Hannah Sanderson, current student; David Lewis, Blended Learning Support Manager.

From external organisations: Peter Gill, Matthew Howard, David Williams and Chris Williams of Graffeg, for unstinting professional support and guidance; Media Wales Ltd, Publishers of Western Mail and Echo, for kind permission to use the Gren cartoon of 1975; East Ayrshire Council, for kind permission to use photographs of Glenbuck, Ayrshire; Gary Jackson, The Troggs Official Website, for kind permission to use the Troggs photograph; John Rogers, Lecturer at Crosskeys College, for the kind copy of the publication 'From Crumlin to Crosskeys'; Glamorgan Archives colleagues, for the professional service and assistance provided and permission to use images of Forest House, 1913 prospectus, coat of arms, brass die, and the beam engine in its original location; People's Collection Wales for permission to use the images of the Swansea Blitz; Brian Davies and colleagues at Pontypridd Museum, for assistance with picture research and a copy of the Foundry Class photograph; Graham Pitcher, 1970s Student Union President, for extensive personal recollections and stories, and use of current photograph; Rhondda Cynon Taff Digital Archive, for kind permission to use photographs of collieries; Natural History Museum, for use of the Iguanodon image. Finally, my thanks to Peter McIntyre, for his unending support and his happy approach to strange errands.